LIVING THE INTENTIONAL LIFE!

So, teach us to number our days, that we may cultivate and bring to You a heart of wisdom. Psalm 90:12

GABRIELLE GAIL DAVIS

@Copyright 2023 - Gail Davis

All rights reserved. This book is protected by the copyright laws of the United States of America. This book may not be copied or reprinted for commercial gain or profit. The use of short quotations or occasional page copying for personal or group study is permitted and encouraged. Unless otherwise identified, Scripture quotations are from the Amplified Version of the Bible. Used by permission. All right reserved.

I dedicate this book to the body of Christ. We are called to be a nation of kings and priest! To my sons Kev, Kay and Keenan. Greatness is your portion! To my daughters, I asked; God gave.

To my grandchildren (Legacy)

To the Kingdom Living Family and Kingdom Connections Fellowship

God has made all of you intentionally great!

Acknowledgment Page

What people are saying about Gabrielle Gail Davis

As spiritual mother and overseer, there's not enough room for the proper accolades she deserves. She stands out among many ministry peers.

Apostle Dr. Veter Nichols-Shaw

Dr. Gabrielle Gail is a true powerhouse and anointed teacher! I've benefited in both the marketplace and kingdom arena!

Holly Davis- Over the top transportation, owner

You always know how to teach where the youngest to the eldest comprehends and benefits! Thank you!   Morrisa Gray

Love you, Mom! Dr. Chenelle Price

TABLE OF CONTENTS

Introduction……………………………………….......6

Chapter One: Live Life Intentionally …………………....9

Chapter Two: Intentionally move from Good to Better……………………………………………..24

Chapter Three: Past pains are meant to produce purpose, not prisons………………………………… …….33

Chapter Four: See it before you see it. ……………………45

Chapter Five: Intentionally work as the Ant works. (Can work unsupervised) …………………………….....62

Chapter Six: Embrace the Good life, by embracing the God Life …………………………………………….....69

Chapter Seven: Avoiding Toxic Relationships. Lessons from Samson ……………………………………………..79

Chapter Eight: Let Go and Let God restore the dreamer in you …………………………………………....…..92

Chapter Nine: It's Your due season! Grab it and don't let go! ……………………………………………………....104

Conclusion………………………………………...161

INTRODUCTION

"Enter through the narrow gate. For wide is the gate and broad and easy to travel is the path that leads the way to destruction and eternal loss, and there are many who enter through it. But small is the gate and narrow and difficult to travel is the path that leads the way to [everlasting] life, and there are few who find it. (Matthew 7:13-14 AMP).

I recently gave a talk to a group of middle school students on: " Don't let your life be a waste of time." "Don't just drift through life." "To live a life that is intentional rather than haphazard." I told them, as one piece of advice I provided them is: "Live with meaning and intention." That is, in my opinion, among the most valuable lessons anyone can learn, and the earlier we realize it, the better.

Implementing the concept of intentional living is one technique to develop and structure your goals to give your life meaning. If you are like myself and many others, you might question. "What is intentional living?" "Why should I make an effort to live deliberately?" Well, I am pleased you enquired because there are numerous benefits and reasons to consider adopting an intentional lifestyle and we'll learn a few of them in this book. The concept of living an intentional life is both liberating and exciting, as it allows you to identify and bring direction and purpose to your life while also allowing you to live your best life knowing God. It makes your objectives as well as resolutions more than just mere words by helping you remember them even after the new year has passed.

Living an intentional life is a notion that aims to make you more conscious of what you do and why you do it. This can be applied to any element of your life, including school, work, family, relationships, and most importantly your relationship with God. All of this is designed to help you become more aware of your options, allowing you to live the full life you desire. Living purposefully can help you realize your goals and stay responsible for yourself and others, whether you have short or long-term ambitions.

At the start of each year, many people declare New Year Resolutions and objectives as a means of improving themselves and be extensively better in the next year and for the foreseeable future. Although, goals and resolutions can be declared at any time, they are most typically professed and discussed at the start of the year. While many resolutions and goals are formed with the best of intentions, many are little more than mere words on a page that are forgotten a week into the new year or a few days later. Actually, the vast majority of individuals completely forget their resolutions and goals, never looking at them again once they have been written down. So, why do many individuals spend time and effort to declare and write down resolutions, just to forget them within a few weeks?

Everybody has a life motto, and apparently, I have mine too, but unfortunately, I was initially missing the objective. I would push the snooze button once, twice, or three times when the alarm went off. I had repeatedly dragged myself out of bed and into the bathroom for my morning routine, assuring myself it was going to be an amazing day. I would commute to work, arrive at work, daydream a little, work some more, and then depart, while keeping an eye fixated on the time. Then bedtime came and it was time to sleep, and the cycle begins all over again the subsequent day. Day-to-day, repeatedly, I was just going through the motions of life, on autopilot. There wasn't very much difference, not a lot of life, and I was mostly reacting to events. Yes, there were some wonderful times when I got to spend time with my family and friends, have a enjoyable meal out or a movie, read a good book, or take a peaceful trip. Beyond paying the bills, those were lovely, momentary diversions, fleeting moments; but there was no permanent joy, no determination to drive me or maintain my interest. And I would constantly contemplate, what to do in my disapproving situations, what exactly is the precise purpose of my existence, do I get a degree and other credentials, and a job with a good salary. And finally, I find myself questioning my subconsciousness on what exactly is living life, and how dire it is that I have allowed myself to live amid adversity and crisis.

So, if you're having difficulties deciding how to prioritize your time and activities, consider if what you are presently doing is fulfilling God's will in your life. If you are uncertain, pray about it. He is desperate to lead you in the right path.

Therefore, be very careful how you live—not as an unwise person, but as a wise person who makes the most of every chance because the days are evil. As a result, do not be foolish, but rather understand what the Lord's will is.

In my search for meaning and passion, I discovered **Living the Intentional Life**.

CHAPTER ONE

Live Life Intentionally

What is Intentional Living

Being deliberate about something is what it means to be intentional. It entails taking full responsibility for one's own life and actions.

INTENT = a decision to act in a specific manner, Resolve
RESOLVE = stands for "firmness of purpose." Resoluteness
RESOLUTENESS = is defined as evidenced by firmness of character or purpose. Determined to do or achieve something; firmness of purpose.

Therefore, with the help of these definitions, I found this statement about living the intentional life to be quite appropriate. The goal is pursued with tenacity and consistency until the intended result is achieved. I came up with the phrase ***"Living the Intentional Life"*** to make it easier to remember: "An intentional life encompasses purpose, discipline, and vision." Let's look at what it means to live an intentional life with these phrases in mind.

When you live intentionally, you do things with intention. For everything and every action, there is a reason, a motivation, and a goal. The first thing I discovered was that there is no such thing as a finish line, no point of arrival. If you live your life with conviction and purpose, you will always be moving, reinventing, and changing; as a result, you will always be growing and evolving.

Don't misconstrue this as me saying there isn't joy, calmness, or contentment in life. It simply implies that you are striving to be a better version of yourself than you were yesterday. When I realized I had been living my life on autopilot, I decided I wanted more from it and stated that I would live consciously rather than allowing life to lead me about. I stated that I would live a spirit-led, meaningful life, being deliberate in how I moved through and showed up in it.

Let us first explore why this is such a significant issue before moving on to the most essential factor. It's easy to fix: If we don't create our agenda for our lives, it will be imposed on us—either by life's events or by other people. To put it another way, living on purpose is the same as living intentionally. It means we're taking charge of our lives and deciding how we'll spend our time, energy, and money. Life can easily "get away from us" and leave us at its mercy if we don't have a strategy in place. I don't believe God intended for us to live like this.

First and foremost, I want to create the groundwork for living the intentional life by addressing the reality that God has always acted in a deliberate/purposeful/intentional manner.

Before the world began, God had a plan.

Your eyes have seen my unformed substance; And in Your book were all written the days that were appointed for me, when as yet there was not one of them [even taking shape]. (Psalm 139:16 AMP).

Declaring the end and the result from the beginning and from ancient times the things which have not [yet] been done, Saying, 'My purpose will be established, And I will do all that pleases Me and fulfills My purpose,' (Isaiah 46:10 AMP).

Just as [in His love] He chose us in Christ [actually selected us for Himself as His own] before the foundation of the world, so that we would be holy [that is, consecrated, set apart for Him, purpose-driven] and blameless in His sight. In love (Ephesians 1:4 AMP).

God's design encompasses every aspect of existence. We live segmented lives in which each of us have our own spiritual life, home life, leisure time, office life, education life, and so on.

God, on the other hand, makes no distinction between the various aspects of our lives. He's concerned about everything. As a result, we can see that God's plan was laid out before the earth even existed, and it encompasses all aspects of life. God's plan will undoubtedly be carried out.

The Lord of hosts has sworn [an oath], saying, "Just as I have intended, so it has certainly happened, and just as I have planned, so it will stand. (Isaiah 14: 24 AMP).

Once again, God's plan for the world was set out before the earth even existed; it incorporates every aspects of existence and is guaranteed to be accomplished.

"For everything comes from God alone, everything lives by His power, and everything is for His Glory." Romans 11:36 (TLB)

If you want to fulfill your destiny, you must learn to live life on intention! You must quit allowing fear to intentionally suffocate your faith, deter your courage and ultimately destroy your intents. Instead, eradicate fear from your life with faith and an unsurmountable courage. Fortunately, this can be easily achieved by doing exactly what you are afraid of! Doing what instills that ludicrous fear in you. Doing what you're afraid of isn't just doing things on the spur of the moment. No! The importance of preparation and timing cannot be overemphasized.

The First step is preparation through wisdom and instruction. This will calm many fears. Heed direction from God by simply turning to Him in prayer.

Now, His response could take a variety of forms. Obviously, the Bible can be a means of God's response, dreams or visions can be another means, His audible voice can also be a means of Him responding to you, He can also respond through prophecy, and other means.

However, one thing is certain: it will arrive through your spirit's voice of serenity says (Proverbs 25:2 EXB), *"God is honored for what He keeps secret [It is the glory of God to hide a matter/ thing;*

Also, the bible says in *(Deut 29:29), "The secret things belong to the LORD our God, but the things which are revealed and disclosed belong to us and to our children forever, so that we may do all of the words of this law"*.

The above bible passages all portray an important thing that I want you to learn, brethren: be rest assured that God has a plan for your life that is now unfolding. It might appear faint now, but be confident that he never forgets and he remembers every plan he has in store for you.

You may even forget a prior prayer, but God does not forget. You will definitely receive an answer from him. All we have to do now is put our faith in him. Joshua 1:1-9 is a fascinating story that illustrations how you must rise above your circumstances and follow the heavenly path laid out before you. Joshua had to make a decision. After 40 years in the wilderness, Moses, his leader, and his example had passed away, and now God is commanding Joshua to rise. To be successful, we must learn from our forefathers. Joshua's life possessed hope and destiny. Destiny is on your side, just as it is on mine. In verse 7, which is an important scripture to remember, the bible says, "*Only be strong and courageous, so you may perform according to all the law that Moses, my servant, told you; do not depart from it to the right hand or to the left hand, that you may flourish wherever you go.*"

Why did God specify that the right hand or the left hand should be used? Because the hands are symbols of power, control, and possession. After a certain age, you have power, authority, and ownership over the decisions you make for your life. You are on the divine path of intentional prosperity when you let God's hand order your movements.

"Beloved, I pray that in every way you may succeed and prosper and be in good health [physically], just as [I know] your soul prospers [spiritually]. (3 John 1:2). "For I know the plans and thoughts that I have for you,' says the Lord, 'plans for peace and well-being and not for disaster, to give you a future and a hope. declares the Lord (Jeremiah 29:11). All you have to do is be brave and strong. To put it another way, don't be circumspect. Allowing fear to paralyze you, propagating falsehood, and dictating your actions is not something you should do.

Joshua's personal Goliath, The Hittites, would have to be faced for him to reach his promised land. The Hittites were descendants of Heth, whose name means "terror," and the word terror alludes to the most severe form of fear, especially concerning the unknown element. "Things you can't see with your eyes" (shamah-elim.info June 2004). The Hittites are a personal Goliath that all great men and women must battle. However, confronting it will strengthen your faith, from good to great. As an illustration, consider the following:

Do you know someone who has had a bad relationship or had been deeply wounded in church, and you have heard them repeatedly saying, "I am done with relationships" or "I am never going back to that church?" Of course, the goal is to never feel the pain they have previously encountered, and even more importantly, to never face the possibility of feeling such sorrow or disappointment. I used to have a friend like that. In fact, he promised not to return to church, despite his love for the Lord, and to never enter into a long-term relationship, despite his desire to have a family. He was struggling with vulnerability's Goliath.

Love has its level of vulnerability, as well as the "unknown" things that your intellect can't perceive. However, these vulnerabilities can be conquered by recognizing your Goliath and confronting him head-on while admitting God's sovereignty; the battle belongs to the Lord and victory to you.

This is something you will hear me say a lot in this book; the number 40 is a significant number. The Philistine champion Goliath harassed Israel's children for 40 days. Daily, he taunted them with his presence, both verbally and visibly. The number 40 denotes a period of probation or testing. David refused to be overwhelmed by fear. But how did he do it? He rehearsed his prior successes, dismissed his critics, and put his faith in God.

We must do the same, regardless of what situation we are in, to live an intentionally victorious life, we must remember and practice our wins. Ignore the critics, whether they are friends, family, or your internal voice of past failures, and trust in the Almighty God. Thankfully, my friend eventually followed David's example and is now married to a woman who adores him and he is happily back in the church.

What You Should Know About Living an Intentional Life.

When you live your life with intention, you have direction and purpose to help you achieve the life that you want to live. This way of living also creates an environment for growth, peace, and happiness. It forces you to reflect on your current life and make the necessary changes to get you to live the life you want.

Intentional living does not imply that you have everything planned out for the rest of your life right now. Even if you don't have every detail of your life sorted out, living an intentional life means that you live with a purpose; that you have a reason for all you do.

It's important to remember while implementing an intentional living lifestyle that you can choose to be intentional about the path you want your life to go even if you don't know where you will end up. Even if you don't have all the details figured out, having a concept of where you want your life to go and what you want to achieve in your life can offer you a beginning point, and an off point. This allows you to begin working toward your ultimate end goals while all the minor details are ironed out along the road.

Your basic beliefs, which influence how you pick the path your life will take, are the driving force behind intentional living. This means that, while you don't need to have your entire life planned out, you do need to know what matters most to you. Each person's essential values will be distinct from another. Most people's underlying values are influenced by society, their families, religious beliefs, and even what they see on television and in the media. Dedication, sincerity, commitment, open-mindedness, and reliability are examples of core values. My values include, among other things, my relationships with others, my family, and my creator. Knowing my basic principles have enabled me to live a more purposeful life. Assuring that my decisions lead me to the accomplishment of the objectives I have set for myself and my future.

If you are not sure what your basic values are, take some time to reflect on some happy or proud experiences in your life.

Take advantage of these opportunities to explore a little further. Consider the things in your life that are most important to you. Do you find it difficult to form and maintain relationships with others? Are values like honesty, integrity, loyalty, and godliness essential to you? What characteristics do you think you possess? Most people feel joy and pride when they live and behave according to their core values, which helps them to align their life with what they believe is most important. You can use this as a roadmap to align your decisions as you navigate your life to achieve your life goals.

You may start living an intentional life once you have figured out what your basic values are. Using your core values and beliefs as a moral compass to guide you on the right path and keep you focused on what matters most to you in life.

How To Live an Intentional Life

There are a few simple measures you can incorporate in your daily life to help you begin living life with purpose/intention. These steps are as follows:

1. Take a personal inventory of yourself. What makes you, you.

2. Set daily goals and monitor what you do daily. What you do daily is an indication of what your future holds.

3. Redeem Time by valuing it more.

4. Self-Death daily.

5. Lean on Grace.

6. Carry Out the Expedient.

7. Leave Yourself Open.

8. Plant Seeds.

9. Accept the Process as It is.

Taking Personal Responsibility: The most important aspect of living intentionally is accepting responsibility for your choices and outcomes. Because life is unpredictable, even the best-laid plans don't always work out the way we expect or hope. It is critical to accept responsibility for how you will respond to situations beyond your control at these times. For example, are you going to let the failure of getting the dream job you applied for keep you from looking for other jobs and ultimately transform yourself into a couch potato living in your parent's basement? Or are you going to take what you have learned and apply for other jobs, putting yourself out there in the hopes of finding something greater than what you were looking for in the first place?

Essentially, it would practically become easier for you to adjust to the hiccups that you encounter on your life's journey that disturb your plans when you understand how to accept responsibility and adjust to the various hiccups, twists, and turns life throws your way. Taking personal responsibility for your life is the simplest way to respond and act to the different curveballs that life tends to throw your way.

Set Goals: The end to which effort is directed is one's definition of a goal. According to Apostle Paul, he strives for the prize of the upward call in Christ Jesus. *Not that I have already obtained it [this goal of being Christlike] or have already been made perfect, but I actively press on [a]so that I may take hold of that [perfection] for which Christ Jesus took hold of me and made me His own. Brothers and sisters, I do not consider that I have made it my own yet; but one thing I do: forgetting what lies behind and reaching forward to what lies ahead, I press on toward the goal to win the [heavenly] prize of the upward call of God in Christ Jesus. (Philippians 3:12-14 AMP).*
He had a certain objective in mind. If you don't have any goals you're striving to attain, you're like footballers playing football without a touchdown line or soccer players kicking the ball

around the field without goalposts. Goal-setting also entails deciding what one wants to achieve and then devising a plan to achieve it within a specific time range. Nothing is dynamic unless it is first defined.

Redeem Your Time: In life, time is the only commodity that cannot be replaced. It's important to remember that time is a commodity that can be traded. It pays significant benefits when used consistently and wisely. Over time, time spent on good education results in a strong intellect. We value time so highly that when someone takes the time to spend it with us, we express our gratitude. Money can be replaced, but time cannot. To redeem time, we must be diligent and make the most of the possibilities we are given in life. It also entails feeling a sense of urgency about one's task because the days are getting shorter. To get the most out of your time, you must avoid procrastination and inactivity.

Self-Death Daily: *I assure you, believers, by the pride which I have in you in [your union with] Christ Jesus our Lord, I die daily [I face death and die to self]*. As Apostle Paul put it in *(1 Corinthians 15:31)*.
According to Jesus in (Luke 9:23), we should take up our cross and follow Jesus, every day. The crucifixion of our sinful Adamic nature in us is symbolized by the cross.
Daily death is denying our human nature's lusts and appetites (on a daily and recurring basis). It is to stay on the straight and narrow path of self-discipline with the guidance of the Holy Spirit who lives inside us. We can bring God's holiness and glory to our planet by dying every day. *"Always carrying around in the body the dying of Jesus, so that the [resurrection] life of Jesus also may be shown in our body. 11 For we who live are constantly [experiencing the threat of] being handed over to death for Jesus' sake, so that the [resurrection] life of Jesus also may be evidenced in our mortal body [which is subject to death]. 12 So physical death is [actively] at work in us, but [spiritual] life [is actively at work] in you"*. *(2 Corinthians 4:10-12 AMP)*.

Lean On Grace: As defined by someone, grace is God's power made accessible to meet our needs at no cost to us. Grace is a sculptor of men and their fates. *"But by the [remarkable] grace of God, I am what I am, and His grace toward me was not without effect. In fact, I worked harder than all of the apostles, though it was not I, but the grace of God [His unmerited favor and blessing which was] with me". (1 Corinthians 15:10).*
Grace inspires us to do great things for God *(Zechariah 4:6-7)*. Having a determined mind isn't enough to live consciously. His mercy is desperately needed. Even when we fail, God's grace allows us to pick ourselves up, dust ourselves off, and keep going. *"For a righteous man falls seven times, and rises again, But the wicked stumble in time of disaster and collapse". (Proverbs 24:16).*

Carry Out the Expedient: The useful and productive activities that we engage in are expedient things. We develop excellent habits by doing the expedient regularly. According to psychologists, changing a behavior takes 30 days. The convenient is the polar opposite of the expedient, and it rarely yields positive results. Doing what is handy consistently is equivalent to developing bad habits that will never produce amazing results. Success is not the result of a single occurrence; rather, it is the result of a series of efficient actions.

Leave Yourself Open: *"For David, after he had served the purpose of God in his own generation, fell asleep and was buried among his fathers and experienced decay [in the grave];" (Acts 13:36, AMP).*
In *(Mark 10:45)*, Jesus stated that he came to serve, not to be served, and to sacrifice his life as a ransom.
You will never be remembered for what you receive; instead, you will be recognized for what you give. To live consciously means to serve your generation according to God's will. Every year, look for ways to serve in your family, church, or community.

Plant Seeds: Planting a seed is the basis of the law of reproduction. *"While the earth remains, Seedtime and harvest, Cold* *and heat, Winter and summer, and day and night Shall not cease."* (*Genesis 8:22 AMP*).

Every seed reproduces in the same manner as the one before it. Planting seeds for what you want to harvest is the essence of an intentional life. Farmers plant seeds with intention. If a farmer does not plant during the planting season, there will be nothing to harvest during the harvest season. Prudent farmers do not eat their entire crop. Every harvest contains seeds for the following planting season, and the size of the following harvest is determined by the number of seeds sown. To your advantage, believe this principle: to your detriment, ignore it.

Accept the Process as It Is: It's vital to realize that adopting an intuitive lifestyle isn't something that happens suddenly. It's a process, a personal trip that takes time but produces incredible results. Although there is no end destination or finish line to reach, it is all about making and applying minor changes throughout your life: modifying your way of thinking to align with the life you want to live.

After I hit an unprecedented low in my life, I came up with the idea and practice of living an intentional life. I was in my early thirties, a mother of three and on the brink of a divorce.

In life, we all have had dreams and expectations for the future, including work, family, and life in general. It was not until I became jobless after losing my job that I invested my years in more important and profitable ventures. Armed with a bachelor's degree that was more of a liability than an asset because my work experience superseded the degree, I was forced to reconsider my life and what I wanted from it.

For the first week or so, I didn't eat much and didn't sleep much; I was barely surviving daily. But it was not until I discovered I had the power to turn my situation around that I knew I could. I couldn't expect to wake up the next day with my dream job, but I could do small things to help me to get closer to discovering and landing it.

I began by focusing on minor tasks which I had control over, such as making my bed, doing my laundry, and even picking what to eat for dinner. These modest gestures provided me with the impetus I needed to look beyond my current circumstances and make plans for the future. I understood I had to seek employment, even though it wasn't something I wanted to do for my entire life. What happened was that I was able to get a temporary position, and through that job, I was able to make contacts that helped me land a career in the future that was similar to the one I had been looking for.

All of this was feasible because I asked myself, "why?" Why was I in this situation in the first place, and why did I want to get out? I was able to build a plan of living intentionally after I learned the answers to these questions, allowing me to turn my life into what I want. It began with me identifying my basic beliefs, strengths, and weaknesses and determining what I eventually desired from my life. It isn't difficult to learn to live an intentional life, but it does take some time and effort on your part. You must be willing to make a change or a series of changes, as well as live with a sense of purpose. Stop doing things merely for the sake of doing them and start doing things because you have a reason to. Making my bed every day was a high point for me since it was the one thing in my life that I had control over at that time, and it set the tone for the rest of the day.

Creating an Intentional Lifestyle

Once you make the decision, incorporating an intentional lifestyle into your daily existence is relatively simple. It starts with a desire to raise your existing life to what it can be, and eventually what you want it to be. Begin by asking yourself tough questions about why you do what you do and what you want to do and achieve in your life. "Where do you see yourself in the next five years?" "Where do you see yourself in the next ten years?" This is a common question that everyone encounters as they grow up and approach adulthood. Ask yourself where you see yourself and your life going using this mode of questions. Do you envision yourself being called to serve in God's vineyard as a Pastor, an Apostle, or a missionary? Do you envisage yourself as a retired millionaire living on a private island, or as the CEO of a multi-million-dollar company?

You must not only choose the path in which you want your life to travel, but you must also determine the "why" behind your final vision. Why are you interested in retiring on a private island? Why are you interested in being God's Servant? What motivates you to aspire to be the CEO? Why do you want your company to be a multi-million-dollar one? Why do you see yourself as the person you aspire to be in the future?

Furthermore, it's also vital to desire explaining the why behind the choices and decisions you make in your life. It's essential to remember that people's opinion about the way you live your life doesn't matter. Most individuals are too preoccupied with creating a life that others would approve of, rather than attempting to live their best lives. When you concentrate on your own life, you have less time to be concerned about what others are accomplishing or contemplating, and you are better able to achieve your objectives; living an intentional life.

My Challenge to You

Since you have learned a little more about living an intentional life, I hope you will be encouraged to put it into practice in your life, as I have done in mine. Set life objectives, figure out what your "why" is, and see what you can do to get what you want out of life. Determine your life's "why" and make it happen! Set yourself up for some minor victories, small tasks that you can complete with little effort daily. This gives you more confidence in your decision to live a more intentional life and in your ability to achieve the goals you have set for yourself with the help of the Holy Spirit.

It's important to remember that living an intentional lifestyle isn't a checklist to be completed. It's a never-ending process that changes and evolves as your life goals and thoughts evolve. Continue to question yourself "why" you do or want things in your life and be satisfied with your responses. This will lead to you living an intentional life with a distinct purpose. A life that is tailored to follow God's path for you and your goals in life. Live life intentionally every day!

CHAPTER TWO

Intentionally move from Good to Better

"The day you find someone as committed to your objective as you are to hold them accountable is the day you take your first lasting step toward success. Making a goal commitment to your accountability partner will make the milestone more achievable to achieve". Eric Thomas.

Establishing positive intentions decreases tension and substitutes any negative ideas that would otherwise slow us down on our journey from good to better. Moving forth with purpose cultivates a positive mental attitude that allows us to perform at our best.

Why should your good deprive you of your better when your existence is created to move from good to better? You may be in a good situation right now, and for that, you should be grateful. Gratitude serves as a springboard for upward mobility.

People often remark that your gratitude affects your latitude or altitude, but what exactly does this mean? Gratitude is a powerful energy that energizes, motivates, and stimulates people. It adds an upbeat to your step rhythm. Gratitude opens the door to blessings when you actively practice it. As a result, being appreciative in all circumstances is critical. Being conscious of the blessings you already have is the footprint of intentional gratitude, and this is the beginning of success.

In (Matthew 25:23 AMP) *"His master said to him, 'Well done, good and faithful servant. You have been faithful and trustworthy over a little, I will put you in charge of many things; share in the joy of your master.',"*

His master congratulated him. Take pleasure in the Lord's joy. You will be catapulted to gratefulness if you practice gratitude. Gratitude helps you to see things in a new light.

Do you have any areas of your life where you have found a considerable level of comfort? Have you found a sense of accomplishment? You were born with the ability to move forward. That is why you have chosen to read this book.

According to Johann Kaspar Lavater, "there are three types of men: the retrogrades, the stationary, and the progressives," and each and every one of us falls into one of these three categories of men.

The retrogrades are the ones who easily retreats under any uneasy circumstances they're confronted with on their journey to success, the stationary are the immobile ones, scared to fail, scared to try something new, scared to leave their comfort zone and also serial procrastinators. While the progressives as the name entails are the ones willing to make changes and effect changes as the need arises. Always willing to leave their comfort zone and pragmatically obsessed with actualizing their goals and objectives.

The later type of men are the ones who are purpose-driven and are intentionally working to acquire their life's objectives.

Be abreast with the fact that God delights in blessing people with both temporal and spiritual gifts. *"Every good thing given and every perfect gift is from above; it comes down from the Father of lights [the Creator and Sustainer of the heavens], in whom there is no variation [no rising or setting] or shadow cast by His turning [for He is perfect and never changes]"*. *(James 1:17 AMP)*.

Therefore, you must learn to reposition your mindset, intentionally moving from good to better.

Signs That God is Intentionally moving you from Good to Better

You may not realize it, but your current circumstances could be God's method of preparing you for even greater things. Your current condition may be retrograde or stationary, but if you persevere and trust Him, brighter days will come.

Look for the following clues to reveal that God is pushing you into something better to help you recognize His presence in your life.

- **You will have the opportunity to learn new skills or improve your existing ones**: If you have been given the chance to study or enhance a skill, consider why you are devoting time to it. Is learning it just for fun or out of curiosity? Is it because you recognize that it will be useful to you in the near future? If your enthusiasm for that skill grows daily, then it may be intended to be a part of you. How much more once you've mastered that skill? It is not a coincidence that you obtained a skill that required a significant amount of time spent learning it, it requires hard work, and resolute dedication. If God wants you to do something bigger, He will undoubtedly prepare you for it. As a result, place a premium on the skills you have honed.

- **You are subjected to rejections:** A succession of rejections is evidence that God is calling you to something else. Maybe you have been attempting to be a part of a group or organization for a long time. They would not accept you regardless of what you did. Or you may have succeeded in becoming a part of it, but you have always felt out of place. Is this a sign that you have a problem you are oblivious to or because not the best situation for you? God can shut a door that no man can open. What could be the reason He doesn't want you in that group? While you may not know, if you diligently follow his path, you'll definitely not go amiss.

You have lost interest in your present job or profession: Have you unexpectedly ceased being interested in what you are doing, such as your career or ministry? For example, you may have been so devoted to it for a long period that it had become your entire world. Then you abruptly lost interest in it, and it feels like you are dragging your feet simply to keep working. If this is how you are feeling right now, you need to take a look at yourself. It could be an indication that you're burnt out from tiredness, or it could be a sign that you are transitioning to a new season. However, before deciding to quit, evaluate yourself and pray to God for wisdom.

- **You notice new doors opening up in front of you.** The availability of better opportunities is a clear sign that God is moving you from good to better. You can think of this as a foregone conclusion, especially if you have had previous failures or rejections. Of course, you must confirm whether or not it is God's will. Not every good opportunity comes from God. Some are simply designed to divert your attention away from God's true plan for your life. That is why you must be alert to the voice of the Holy Spirit.

- **You meet people who inspire you to strive for greater things:** Another evidence is if you have recently been surrounded by folks who encourage you to pursue bigger dreams. It is not by chance that you run into some folks. There is a concept known as divine connection, and God will allow you to meet people who can help you fulfill your purpose or calling. What are you going to do when you meet these people? They are most likely placed in your life by God so that you can learn from them. He may even utilize them to generate opportunities for you to migrate to a better place.

- **You are being pushed to move by your circumstances.** The situation in which you find yourself can also indicate whether you should go or remain in your status quo. Your circumstances may be used by God to persuade you to obey His instructions. For instance, you may have been compelled to relocate. You, on the other hand, are unlikely to desire to leave your familiar surroundings. As a result, the Lord will permit a catastrophe to occur for you to decide to leave.

Other than God wants to move you by showing signs, it is also important for you to intentionally make an utmost effort to always want to advance. And how you make the move also matters. See below how to leap from good to better.

How to Intentionally Leap from Good to Better

"Be strong and courageous, do not be afraid or tremble in dread before them, for it is the Lord your God who goes with you. He will not fail you or abandon you." (Deuteronomy 31:6).

Because I want to encourage you to see the importance of progressively moving from good to better and making it a priority in your life. The first law is the law of progression. To make and feel progress, consider going the extra inch instead of the extra mile. We don't get better by merely existing. We must be deliberate about it. And the sooner you make the switch to being intentional about your progress, the better: because growth compounds and accelerates when you are. Here is how to make the move:

i. **Now is the time to confront the big question.** The first time I made the conscious decision to progress from good to better, I realized that it would be a lifelong journey. To get to an ultimate destination, my focus shifted from "How long will this take?" to "How far can I go?" That's the question you should be asking yourself right now—not that you'll be able to answer it completely. You might have been on the journey from good to better for several years now and yet no visible success and you might be asking "why". Below are a few points that will assist you in determining the direction, if not the distance of you journey from good to better.

- What do you want to do with your life?
- What path do you wish to take?
- What is the furthest distance you can envisage traveling?

Answering those questions will get you started on your personal improvement journey from good to better. Making the most of whatever you have been given is the best you can hope for in life. You achieve this by investing in yourself and striving to be the best version of yourself. The more resources you have at your disposal, the bigger your potential—and the further you should strive to go. "To whom much is given—much shall be asked," my father used to say to me when I was a child. Give it your all to become the finest version of yourself.

ii. **Confront Your Fears.** *"So do not be afraid because I am with you; do not be alarmed for I am your God. I will strengthen and assist you; with my righteous right hand, I will uphold you". (Isaiah 41:10).*

I recently read an article on how people's worries prevent them from progressing from good to better. The following five factors influenced the outcome:

- The Fear of failing.
- The Fear of sacrificing safety for the unknown.

- Fear of being financially overstretched.
- Concerns about what others may say or think.
- Fear of alienating peers as a result of your success.

Which of these anxieties had the greatest impact on you? It was the last one for me: alienating my peers. I'm a people pleaser by nature, and I wanted everyone to like me. But it doesn't matter which fear has the greatest impact on you. We all have been afraid of something at one point but what your belief system (Faith) is will supersede fear if you allow it. "Which feeling will you permit to be stronger?" You must ask yourself because the stronger emotion wins, and your response is critical. I want to inspire you to nourish your faith while starving your fears. When you are able to overcome your fear of stagnation and embrace development, the sky will unquestionably become your starting point for being better.

iii. **Turn from Unintentional to Intentional Growth.** People tend to get stuck in the "rut" of life with distractions, circumstances, or even some day-to-day routines. They just get by after a while. It's only because of some sort of happenstance or an unforeseen accident or incident that they gain new knowledge or are forced to do something different. Make sure that doesn't happen to you! If that's your mindset, keep in mind that the only difference between a rut and a grave is the length!

How can you tell if you have been stuck in a rut? Consider the following distinctions between unintentional and intentional growth:

UNINTENTIONAL	INTENTIONAL
Waiting for tomorrows Plans	Insists on Getting Started Right Now
Waiting for Growth to Arrive	Takes full responsibility for his or her development
Only by making mistakes can one learn.	Frequently learns before making a mistake
He or She is dependent on good fortune.	Hard work is important to him or her.
Early and frequent quitting	Long and arduous perseverance
Adopts Bad Habits	Fights for Good Habits
Has a lot to say	Maintains Consistency
Takes the Safe Route	Takes Chances
Assumes the Role of a Victim	Thinks like a student
Depends on Talent	Depends on Personality
After graduating, he or she stops learning.	Never Stops Getting Better

"One's philosophy is best stated in words; it is expressed in the decisions one takes," Eleanor Roosevelt observed. In the end, we are the ones who shape our lives and ourselves. The cycle will continue till we die. And we are ultimately responsible for the decisions we make.

You must do much more than simply live life and hope to learn what you need along the way if you want to fulfill your full potential and become the person you were designed to be. As if your future depended on it, you must go out of your way to seize growth possibilities. Growth does not happen by itself—not for me, not for you, and not for anyone else. It's up to you to go after it!

(Luke 8:14-15 NIV) says, *"The seed that fell among thorns stands for those who hear, but as they go on their way they are choked by life's worries, riches and pleasures, and they do not mature. But the seed on good soil stands for those with a noble and good heart, who hear the word, retain it, and by persevering produce a crop".*

Be ecstatic if you have realized that God is pushing you to actively move from good to better. The approach may not be easy or painless, but it is well worth the effort. Set out in trust and follow God's lead. You will undoubtedly find yourself in a position that you previously only fantasized about.

CHAPTER THREE

Past pains are meant to produce purpose, not prisons.

We all experience pain in life, whether emotional or physical pain. No pain is alike, we must all walk the journey and path that God has destined for our lives, yet God promises that there is a purpose in all pain. We can press on each day knowing that our God loves us and wants to use the hurt and pain in this world to glorify Himself. The below Bible verses can help you understand the purpose of pain in your life and encourage you to find joy in the midst of suffering. Please, don't give up hope. God has so much more in stock for your life as we ponder on this chapter.

"For I know the plans and thoughts that I have for you,' says the Lord, 'plans for peace and well-being and not for disaster, to give you a future and a hope." (Jeremiah 29:11 AMP).

"The Lord is close to the brokenhearted, and he delivers those whose spirit has been crushed." (Psalm 34:18 ISV)

"And God will wipe away every tear from their eyes; there shall be no more death, nor sorrow, nor crying. There shall be no more pain, for the former things have passed away." (Revelation 21:4)

Many people are ignorant of their potential until they are confronted with their suffering. We can only eliminate what we are confronted with. We can express abilities that have been suppressed for a long time while we are in pain. We get stronger as a result of our experiences with pain. Some individuals simply get by in life, but conquering your pain allows you to progress.

Have you ever found yourself chastising yourself for past choices? Are you still wounded from past breakups? What if you're still walking in an offense you can't seem to get out of? Have you been subjected to physical or emotional abuse? All, or at least the majority, of those incarcerations, have been dealt with by me. Allow me to share at least a few stories from my life's history book.

Following my previous divorce, I found myself as a single mother attempting to preserve the lifestyle that my children and I had become accustomed to. We didn't live this lavish lifestyle when married, but as the saying goes, *"Two are better than one because they have a more satisfying return for their labor;" (Ecclesiastes 4:9 AMP)*. My ex, unfortunately, did not extend a hand to help financially to support our children despite a court ruling. So, I started making "gourmet" meals out of Ramen Noodles, one piece of meat, and a bag of frozen vegetables. For secondhand toys, I shopped Black Friday bargains at secondhand retailers like the Salvation Army (By the way, the fact that most of them were missing components or broken in some manner today makes us laugh.) I bought my work clothing from Goodwill, which also doubled as church clothes, and I only had three pairs of shoes: black, navy blue, and brown, which had to suffice for both church and work. My rage and tears were fueling my motivation at the time. How could my ex-husband just go about his business, unconcerned by the fact that we were now crammed into a two-bedroom apartment and struggling?

Please, God, hear my screams and see my tears!! And believe me when I say this: God did it! He assisted and shouldered me in getting unstuck and avoiding hopelessness. Determined to reclaim and, if possible, exceed status, I outlined what Mommy needed to do for us to get ahead, as well as what they needed to do to assist and shoulder the load. The cost: returning to school while working a full-time job and having no social life other than Sunday morning church. The lesson learnt is that to gain, one must give up something.

It wasn't long until I was able to find a better-paying job and become the sole owner of a four-bedroom, 3724-square-foot home, earning three times my previous wage. My suffering resulted in a promise that was just waiting to happen. The closer it gets to your promise, the more uncomfortable things are, just like a pregnant woman. It is estimated that having a baby will take 40 weeks which is also the time for testing and probation. A pregnant woman must overcome any feelings of abandonment or abandoning the pregnancy, she must nourish the promise, adjust to the obvious changes that are occurring, and keep her focus on the promise by continually making preparations.

Then, she is finally ready to take possession of the promise by giving birth to it. That did not come without a cost. Finally, her final examination has arrived. Barring down to push through her anguish, her urge to give up, and to travel through what some refer to as the ring of fire, none of which is easy. But, in the end, she has given birth to hope, purpose, and increase. However, if transformation and repositioning does not come with it, she won't see herself for who she has become. She had a child and was a mother. rather, she will see herself for what she was becoming.

It will be painful until you comprehend the reason for your suffering.
"If our lives are always simple, it is because we have been called to a lesser purpose," Rick Joyner stated.

PAIN and **PURPOSE** have a symbiotic relationship. Your purpose is masked by your suffering. Your anguish will continue to be painful until you recognize the reason behind it.

Have you ever considered why you are in pain? Have you ever tried to figure out what your pain is for? If everything is working in your favor, you must accept that suffering, as unpleasant as it may be, is also working in your favor.

We all have to go through hardships in our lives, but not everyone would find meaning in their suffering.

Amidst agony, you must make two essential decisions: the first is to decide what to do in your pain, and the second is to decide what to do with your pain.

The first is about you, while the second is about other people. Suffering is a choice, but pain is unavoidable. You may either wallow in your grief for the rest of your life or you can choose to turn it around and put it to good use. Which one would you rather choose?

Several people miss out on their purpose because they spend their life attempting to prevent or protect themselves from pain. Pain does not destroy a person; rather, it shows who he is.

As a matter of fact, the more difficult a problem is to solve, the more discoveries you make along the way.

Joyce Meyer detailed how she was physically, intellectually, emotionally, and verbally assaulted by her father until she left home at the age of 18 in one of her writings, Life Beyond Abuse. She described how her father repeatedly raped her at least 200 times.

The emotional turmoil, pain, and fear left an indelible mark on her self-esteem, but it's incredible how this same woman has grown over the years to write countless articles and books on abuse, self-esteem, confidence, forgiveness, rejection, gratitude, fear, addiction, and habits; topics gleaned from her raw experience in overcoming her childhood abuse.

We must see our suffering through the eyes of God's plan.

"It's not our experiences that make or break us," Mark Batterson stated. Who we become is ultimately determined by our interpretation of an explanation for those experiences. Your explanations take precedence over your experiences."

Allowing the ambiguity of your pain to cloud the clarity of the purpose it can serve in your life is a mistake.

Every terrible experience can be used by God for a good cause. Ask yourself these questions to help you find meaning in your suffering: How could my experience of suffering bring hope to someone else who needed to hear it? What effect has my anguish had on my attitude toward others who are in agony? What can I make or generate that will serve as a source of inspiration for others? What is it about my pain that makes me want to change the way I live my life? How is my pain motivating me to make the most of the time I have left? In my suffering, what is God saying to me? Your pain could continue until you understand the message in your pain.

Viktor Emil Frankl was a survivor of the Holocaust. Frankl founded Logotherapy, a psychotherapeutic technique that argues that a lack of meaning is the root of all suffering, stress, and psychiatric illnesses and that the crisis of meaninglessness is the basis of all human problems.

Frankl survived the Holocaust despite spending time in four Nazi death camps from 1942 to 1945, including Auschwitz, but his parents and other family members died in the camps.

"Abandon all hope, ye who enter here," read the plaque at the gate of the feared Nazi death camp of Auschwitz, which was meant to kill a man "little" even before he entered the camp.

Frankl was able to exercise the most crucial freedom of all—the freedom to determine one's attitude and spiritual well-being in any situation—even in the deplorable and abject agony of a concentration camp. No nasty Nazi guard could take that away from him or control Frankl's inner life.

Thinking of the meaning of his suffering was one of the ways he found the fortitude to struggle to stay alive and not lose hope. Frankl recognized that individuals who had nothing to live for died the most quickly in the concentration camps.

Frankl developed a groundbreaking technique of psychotherapy called logotherapy as a result of his suffering in the concentration camp. The belief that humanity's primary motivational force is to seek meaning in every situation is at the heart of this theory, and the work of the logotherapist is to assist the patient in finding personal meaning in life, no matter how bleak the pain or circumstances may be, is at the heart of this theory.

Meaning can be discovered in three ways, according to logotherapy: by making a work or doing a deed; by experiencing something or meeting someone; and by our attitude toward inescapable hardship.

Viktor later wrote a book that changed the way we think about pain as a result of his years of suffering. Man's Search for Meaning, his book, has been hailed as the most extensive and important work of literature to emerge from Hitler's concentration camps.

After going through so much anguish, how could he possibly do so much good? In his book "Man's Search for Meaning," he says, "Man's Search for Meaning" provides some context: "The instant suffering finds a meaning, it ceases to be suffering in some manner."

Frankl made use of what he already had (his pain) to create something new (his purpose). Similarly, so can you. There is meaning hidden in the shadows of your suffering that you may not notice right now. We must seek a goal that will last longer than our suffering.

"Life is never rendered miserable by circumstance, but only by a lack of meaning and purpose," Frankl stated in one of his most famous quotes.

"We are taught by pain."

"Those things that hurt, teach," Benjamin Franklin once stated. It is unavoidable to experience pain; however, it is up to you to learn from it. Even the things that cause us pain can teach us something. The pain would continue until we learned our lessons.

Pain Tells Us Everything We Need to Know. Pain has the ability to unveil potentials that are hidden or dormant. Many people are unaware of their potentials until they are confronted with their suffering. Only what we are confronted with is something we can eliminate. We can express abilities that have been suppressed for a long time while we are in pain.

We get stronger as a result of our experiences with pain.

Some individuals simply go through the motions of life, but conquering your pain allows you to evolve. "The world breaks everyone, and afterward many are strong at the broken places," stated Ernest Hemingway.

Often, adversity helps us to uncover a strength we didn't know we had. "Out of suffering have emerged the strongest souls,"

Kahlil Gibran said, "the most massive characters are seared with scars."

We become more creative as a result of our suffering.

"The purpose of every difficult period is to put a demand on our imagination," Wills Damien remarked. The majority of today's innovations are a result of innovative responses to pain and issues.

Pain is an important fact of happiness if you never experienced some sort of pain, you would never recognize happiness. We get happier while we are in pain. "A good life consists not in the absence of hardships, but in the mastery of them," Helen Keller observed. When we master and overcome our anguish, we get a deep sense of fulfillment.

Pain provides us with a sense of purpose. Don't be ashamed of your scars because they serve as beacons for others who are about to strike the same rocks you did. Your messes would quickly turn into a message for you. Your mistakes are slowly but steadily transforming you into a hero. Your difficulties would quickly turn into victories. Your difficulty is assisting you in achieving your goals. Your rage would quickly turn into a source of energy for you. Your scars would transform you into a celebrity one day.

You must adopt a successful pain management strategy. A winning mentality transforms a disaster into a message, wounds into stars, bitterness into 'bitterness,' irritation into fuel, sorrow into ministry, and hardship into progress. Some aches and pains come to strengthen us as we move closer to the frightening "unseen."

Ultimately, I would like you to think about this: When you are on the right PATH, the TRAVEL is worthy of TRAVAIL. Are you on the proper track in your job, your ministry, your relationships, your business, or your location? There are some aches and pains that aren't worth the journey.

How can you find purpose in your pain?

- Makes you think about your life.
- Increases your empathy.
- You become more grateful.
- Inspires.
- Encourages.

Bear in mind that even the scripture mentioned something about the purpose of pain.

Because Christ willingly bore that suffering, believers receive forgiveness and eternal redemption, which is God's purpose for Christ's pain. John 9:1-3 and 11:1-4 record Christ's testimony that pain can come to us so that God might ultimately be glorified.

Suffering may be painful, but it also serves a purpose from God.

The book of Job in the Bible is a story about a God-fearing man who endured excruciating suffering for an extended period. Job, on the other hand, chose to live a life that daily defined: "... nevertheless I know whom I have believed, and am confident that He is competent to keep what I have given to Him until that day," as the Apostle Paul wrote to Timothy from a Roman jail. (II Timothy 1:12).

Job is a lesson for everyone, but especially for those of us who believe that, while suffering brings pain and disadvantage, it can also serve God's purposes. I'm struck by God's continuous insistence that Satan recognize Job's worthiness as I read Job's story. Even after God had allowed Satan to torture Job with "painful wounds," God persuaded Satan to appreciate the "blameless and upright" Job twice in the first two chapters of Job (Job 1:1, 8; 2:3-10). Satan was supposed to admire Job's loyalty to him while he was suffering..., especially while suffering.

Many people now live lives of suffering, either because they believe God does not allow pain, or because they wonder why God would allow them to suffer when they have been faithful to Him. Job's concern for his suffering was not an immediate "Why?" Instead, he wisely responded to his irritated wife's urging to "curse God and die!" by asking, "Shall we accept good from God, and not trouble?" Both before and after the crucifixion, Christ suffered greatly: the perfect Son of God suffered not for his crimes, but for ours because he was willing and the only sacrifice adequate to pay the price for the forgiveness of all mankind's sins... for all time. Since Christ voluntarily experienced that pain, believers receive forgiveness and eternal redemption, which is God's intention behind Christ's suffering.

Christ's experience in John 9:1-3 and 11:1-4 is that suffering can come to us for God to be exalted in the end.

Within and beyond our sorrow, I believe there is always a God purpose. Personal experience, based on John 3:16-17, is my foundation for that persuasion: "For God so loved the world that He gave His One and Only Son, that whoever believes in Him not only will not perish but will have eternal life." God did not bring His Son into the world to condemn it; rather, He sent Him into the world to save it through Him."

God loves us so much that he sent his Son to Earth to be our sacrifice... no matter how bad we have been, no matter how treacherous we have lived. We can't truly appreciate the enormity and strength, the quality and grade of God's love, unless we grasp that message, which begins in Genesis, continues in Job, and is carried through the Old Testament into the New Testament with its Gospels, Epistles, and Revelation.

I believe there is always a purpose hidden somewhere within the agony of our suffering. It's possible that the aim isn't immediately apparent or even directed at us, but it's also possible that it is. However, the goal can also be to communicate a living and instructional message from God to others via ourselves. We can simply be a tool God chooses to use in His efforts to condemn, persuade, trust, admire, and even understand him as Job did. Satan challenges God's righteousness by alluding to the fact that Job only lived as he did because of the blessings on his life but God knew that Job understood God's sovereignty. One point made repeatedly throughout God's word — beginning in Genesis and continuing through Revelation — is that God has been speaking and acting with purpose toward humans since the beginning.

Therefore, believer, check yourself today, confirm any pain or suffering you find, and question God if you must, but know that He has a purpose planted in you that reveals his explicit trust in your ability to bear the load he has brought or allowed to be brought to you. Pray for him to show you the way. Take a look at His magnificent words. Keep a watchful eye on the situation: Revelation isn't always clear and immediate. If you need assistance, look for a Bible-preaching and-teaching church where you can learn more about God's presence in your life.

"Thus says the Lord who made the earth, the Lord who formed it to establish it—the Lord is His name, 3 'Call to Me and I will answer you, and tell you [and even show you] great and mighty things, [things which have been confined and hidden], which you do not know and understand and cannot distinguish". (Jeremiah 33:2-3 AMP).

Jesus understands your pain and how to assist you in overcoming it. He lived, suffered, and died for every one of us so that we would be reconciled back to Him. Jesus came to earth to teach and help us through our tribulations. Our temptations, sufferings, sadness, and afflictions have all been felt by him.

CHAPTER FOUR

See It Before You See It

I would like you to have a clear understanding in something: humans take the initiative once they believe that they can and in themselves.

When you realize that belief must come first, you will know what you need to work on. Most individuals believe that they must achieve something spectacular to believe in themselves. But can I inform you that if you don't primarily believe in yourself, you will never achieve greatness.

The four-minute mile had remained an unbreakable barrier throughout human history, and people had believed it was insurmountable. They truly believed it was impossible to accomplish. As a result, no matter how hard anybody tried, it could never be broken. Everyone said your heart would explode, yet the human body is incapable of doing so.

Roger Bannister, on the other hand, believed it was attainable. And, despite having little reason to believe it, he was able to train, train, train until he ultimately cracked the four-minute mile barrier. Because he was the only one who believed it could be done, he was the only one who did it.

Now comes the interesting section of the narrative: six weeks after he broke the record, another person broke it, and another, and another, and another, until dozens, hundreds, and thousands of individuals had broken it.

If there is anything that had stood in the way of human progress throughout history: that would certainly be belief. And what actually became the difference in the above story?

They believed it was possible because they saw it before they seen it.

This is the most important point I want you to grasp from this subject. You will start putting your efforts into areas that are beneficial once you realize and understand that they are attainable but you must first strengthen and nurture the belief. Learning to believe in oneself is a skill worth mastering.

Listen, I don't need you to think you're remarkable, or that you should be capable of running a four-minute mile; the reality is that Roger Bannister couldn't initially run a four-minute mile, which is why he had to train. But, before he could go out and accomplish it, he needed to believe that his efforts would be rewarded.

If you believe you can't do anything, it's amazing how much your mind will impede you and create a mediocre mindset in you. Eventually, you'll be incapable of doing it. But if you empower yourself to believe that you're absolutely capable of doing anything; that you are the greatest adaptation machine simply by being human: you'll eventually become successful in your quest to achieve goals, growth and improvement in your life.

Should you suddenly realize that your efforts will be rewarded, and you decide to put in the required effort. Bear in mind that it's those individuals who have dared to believe; who have allowed themselves to believe; and who eventually cultivate that belief with zeal who will ultimately attain their reward. Because, they are more concerned with accomplishment than with everything else.

They visualize it, they think about it, and they imagine themselves performing it. They are obsessed with it. And when they do that, they're putting in the effort to improve, they're taking the steps, and they're doing the things necessary to achieve greatness.

And it is in this environment that greatness emerges. It is based on the concept that putting in the time and effort, doing the difficult things, enduring, and pushing through will eventually pay off in the end. But first and foremost, you must trust; trust in God and trust the God in you and you must have unwavering faith. As a result, devote your time and effort to it. If you don't believe that anything is possible to them that believe, I am telling you right now work on your belief system. Nothing can stop you once you have it.

Our mind may either be our best friend or our deadliest enemy, and we can choose which one it will be. One of life's biggest impediments is learning to manage one's thoughts, which may take on a life of its own if left to its own devices. *(Proverbs23:7 AMP)* states that, *"For as he thinks in his heart, so is he [in behavior—one who manipulates]. He says to you, "Eat and drink," Yet his heart is not with you [but it is begrudging the cost]"*.

Try analyzing your mindset or thoughts you've been contemplating if you are not where your life should be at the moment. Every day, our thoughts essentially build our lives, so pay attention to mental assent. Our thoughts cause emotions or feelings, which would in turn drive our behaviors, which in turn produce the outcomes in our lives.

Let us make an intentional effort to live the life of our dreams as we **SEE** the **NEED** and **TAKE** the **LEAD**.

What to do to Set Intentional Goals and End up living Like Jesus!

Therefore, see that you walk carefully [living life with honor, purpose, and courage; shunning those who tolerate and enable evil], not as the unwise, but as wise [sensible, intelligent, discerning people]. (Ephesians 5:15 AMP).

Living the Intentional Life is something I try to accomplish regularly. This includes intentional resting or meditation on occasions. As a Christian and a Bible teacher, I see the necessity of living your principles, especially if they involve pointless things. I am indeed a massive advocate of knowledge, education and wisdom. In reality, learning is how I "de-stress." Reading is a favorite pastime, playing crossword puzzles to enhance my focus has been one of my personal favorites things to do and wisdom is the principal thing according to the word of God so meditation on His word and how is applies to life is crucial.

Numerous word puzzles provide a word bank to assist you in identifying the terms you will need to solve the problem. It would be difficult to know if the term you saw was the one you were looking for if you didn't have access to that word bank. That was when I realized what I'd been missing.

Once you understand the word you're looking for, your thought cooperates with you just to discover it. Your central nervous system will begin to filter away all of the characters that aren't in the word you're searching for and begin screening in all the letters that you are searching for. Priorities also tend to follow this path too.

When you are searching for a particular term from that bank, you may come across another word in that bank. What is the reason for this? Since your mind is always scanning the word library for the words you're looking for among the multitude of characters.

Your mind would only emphasize what you are actively looking for since your subconscious tells it what to look for: there are far too many impulses in the universe for your brain to properly process it all!

You direct your mind on what to search for while reading the word bank. Your body functions both in conjunction with and independently of your mind! This is a great example of how it feels to engage your conscious mind in an activity. As previously stated, the same is true while pursuing your goals.

Maybe you just gaze at the whole crossword, trying to take in too many characters in the expectation of coming up with something different. Perhaps you chose to take a word from the library and search for it in a multitude of characters when suddenly – Boom – you come across it! This seems to be an illustration of your mind reacting to something you've thought about! When we're in "life," it's the same way.

You can help yourself attain your goals by consciously re-exposing yourself to your checklist of objectives. This is exemplified by Jesus. Because He always said what the Father wanted him to say. He never wavered in his focus or lost sight of His aim. Jesus never lost sight of His major objectives: to glorify the Father, to have constant contact with the Father, and to educate people concerning their authority in Him! It's safe to conclude that Jesus never lost track of His own unique life's ambition!

One may re-expose oneself to their ambitions by reviewing them as often as necessary, visualizing oneself attaining them, or deliberately focusing on them throughout the day. This will gradually find its way into your subconscious thinking. Whatever we think about manifests! Your mind will identify possibilities that correlate to or drive you to achieve those goals faster as you proceed through the days, personal experiences, and personal crises. Of course, the same could be true for living in the opposite direction. You know, when you're focused on the here and now, on flesh and lust. Either you are actively living your values or you are passively unaware of what your true values are!

Your brain can be trained to operate for you or against you, in my opinion. Satan desires to sell you lies, and he will try to do so. The world is capable of deception. There are terrible powers eager to persuade you to think lethally — in a way that tortures, governs, and incapacitates you!

Keep in mind that Jesus always said what He wanted to hear, life giving words . He was constantly in agreement, as well as in His Father's will! That's the image we're supposed to walk in! Life, the solution, and continually praising the Father are the words that come to mind.

The majority of people fail to keep their new year's resolutions because they determine their objectives, write them down, and then set them aside. Every day, as much as possible, one should intentionally speak life to those goals by reading them aloud and consciously reflecting on them. It's also crucial to picture oneself achieving said objectives.

There are numerous parts of the scriptures that emphasize the importance of constantly focusing on God's word and not allowing scripture to escape your sight. The same may be said about living intentionally. According to *(Proverbs 28:19 YLT), Whoso is tilling his ground is satisfied [with] bread, and whoso is pursuing vanity, Is filled [with] poverty.*

When God's Word isn't known or respected, people go crazy, according to this verse. The genuinely blessed are those who follow God's rule. The same idea might be used for our objectives. If you don't know what you want to achieve and your decisions don't reflect it, you will lose track of time and miss opportunities. The truth is that if you select your objectives and set them aside, your attention will follow. The "bright shiny item syndrome" eventually becomes more easily distracting. Everything looks like a terrific idea to you, and you can accomplish it all! Only to discover that you can't and that you have spent all of your energy trying!

Surprisingly, neuroscience backs this up. You will have a 90% improvement in obtaining that goal or having a clearer picture of that objective if you spend one hour a day for 180 days intentionally thinking and seeing yourself accomplishing the goal that you want to achieve. In either case, the outcomes are in your favor!

It's critical to live the intentional life, as Jesus demonstrates in the Gospel. We know this is true because the Scripture is the Word of God! However, according to how the Reticular Activity System operates and how God formed our minds, neuroscience validates these discoveries. Shopping for a vehicle is a great way to see how one's Reticular Activity System functions. When you're thinking about buying a vehicle, your subconscious mind will bring that vehicle to your conscious mind whenever it's close by!

"Oh... this vehicle seems to be everywhere," you begin to consider. The truth is that there are no more such vehicles on the streets than there were previously. The only difference now is that you're aware of them. Your mind responded after you told it what to search for. Throughout the day, your brain begins to filter in the cues you introduce through self-talk and meditation. That's also the power of living intentionally and with a singular concentration like Jesus did. Keep in mind that a man with two minds is insecure in all he does (James 1:8).

Because you were unaware that your subconcious mind urges you to unpack and assemble ideals, behaviors or outcomes, the concious mind provides the input and searches for such vehicle, this is an illustration of how your brain functions. You don't instruct yourself to sleep any more than you tell yourself to eat! Take note of how your thoughts, both unconscious and conscious, lead you to action!

Thoughts turn into words, words into deeds, actions turn into behaviors, behaviors turn into your personality, and your personality turns into your ultimate you!

This, I believe, is why God repeatedly encourages us to dwell on His word and tells us, "Do not be afraid." He knew exactly what would corrupt a person's spirit and dwarth his abilities—and he was correct!

You might be wandering if you ever do not live an intentional life with a defined purpose. Your mind will continue to function as mentioned above this is truth. The most crucial distinction is that when you lack sharp concentration or direction, everything might become a road to go along or an opportunity to seize. You'll start to feel like you're treading water rather than making progress toward your objectives.

The scripture says *"So let's keep focused on that goal, those of us who want everything God has for us. If any of you have something else in mind, something less than total commitment, God will clear your blurred vision Dash, you'll see it yet! Now that we're on the right track, let's stay on it." (Philippians 3:15-16 MSG).*

Living the intentional life and exercising awareness to manage it will provide you with more helpful insights, whereas living haphazardly will provide you with potentially more useless information. To return to the word puzzle, this is an illustration of when you discover a word that isn't in the dictionary.

It's easier to achieve your goals successfully and on schedule once you determine what you are concentrating on and look only what you're concentrating on. Consider the last time you worked a crossword puzzle. Isn't it true that everything else became less significant until you finished the puzzle?

The following texts in the Bible also express the same thing: *"So I say to you, ask and keep on asking, and it will be given to you; seek and keep on seeking, and you will find; knock and keep on knocking, and the door will be opened to you. For everyone who [a]keeps on asking [persistently], receives; and he who keeps on seeking [persistently], finds; and to him who keeps on knocking [persistently], the door will be opened".* (Luke 11:9-10 AMP).

I always wondered when I was younger how does a heart think? Whichever way the heart must have thought that's a man, the scripture says *"above all, preserve your heart, for it is the source of everything you accomplish. Keep perversity out of your mouth, and corrupt discourse out of your mouth. Allow your eyes to follow a straight-line front of you, and your sight to be fixed directly in front of you. Consider your footpaths carefully, and be steadfast in all your endeavors. Keep your foot from evil by not turning to the right or left". (Proverbs 4:23-27).*

What is the significance of someones thought life? "Above all else, guard your heart," Solomon told his son, "Because out of it come the issues of life." Because your thoughts are in charge of the rest of your life.

I will tell you who you are and how you live if you tell me what you think. What you believe determines who you are. You are controlled by your thoughts. *"A man is as he thinks in his heart"* (Proverbs 23:7).

Your attitudes are controlled by your thoughts, whether they be positive, negative, good, or bad. Your thoughts are summed up in your attitudes. Your actions are influenced by your attitudes.

That is something that all excellent psychologists will tell you. "Sow a thought, reap an action," someone once remarked. If you sow a good deed, you will reap a habit. Sow a habit, reap a personality. "If you sow a character, you will reap a destiny."

Before you can do something, you must first think about it. Your thoughts influence your attitudes, which influence your behaviors, which influence your accomplishments. It all starts with the way we think. Your accomplishments will be a culmination of your thoughts.

Intentionally avoid the trap of discouragement

I've commanded you to be strong and brave. Don't ever be afraid or discouraged! I am the LORD your God, and I will be there to help you wherever you go. (Joshua 1:9 CEV).

Discouragement is a spirit that arises when you do the right things but receive little or no response. It's one of the devil's tactics for making you feel horrible about yourself, sabotaging your progress, and preventing you from achieving your goals. Discouragement is not something that should be tolerated. It should not be allowed to take hold of us; instead, it must be resisted, and in dealing with it, we must be stern at times and tender at other times. "Let not your heart be worried," Jesus remarked in *(John 14:1 AMP), "Do not let your heart be troubled (afraid, cowardly). Believe [confidently] in God and trust in Him, [have faith, hold on to it, rely on it, keep going and] believe also in Me".*

Discouragement is a "human" temptation *(1 Corinthians 10:13)*. An attack in the soulish realm. And, in dealing with it, we need sensitivity at times and hardness at other times. Discouragement, in any case, should not be accepted or indulged in. It is a battle that must be waged.

It could cost a great deal if we stay discouraged. It depletes our energy and vision by instilling a sense of failure and hopelessness. It can take time to overcome. Because we don't want to face it, it can impede us from doing what we need to accomplish. It can even be infectious, eroding other people's faith.

When we are dejected, we naturally want comfort, which is natural. However, the solaces we seek are frequent strategies to avoid our concerns rather than solutions to summon the fortitude to confront and overcome them. When this happens, discouragement becomes a sinful indulgence in unbelief, similar to a desire, anger, or other unbelief-related sins.

Jesus doesn't want us to be disheartened; in fact, He forbade us from being discouraged because He knew that horrible things would happen.

How can you get rid of discouragement? Look to God's word for guidance. *"For the word of God is alive and powerful, and sharper than any two-edged sword, penetrating even to the dividing of soul and spirit, of joint and narrow, and is a discernment of the thoughts and intentions of the hearts," according to (Hebrews 4:12).*

You may not want to get into God's word when you are disheartened, but you must go against your feelings. Take care of your physical well-being. Eat healthily and sleep soundly. Giving your body the attention, it needs will make you feel less depressed.

Hang out with people who seem to be having a good time. When you spend time with pleasant individuals, you will naturally feel better. Keep your focus on your task. Please don't give up. Keep your eyes fixed on God's promise and plan for your life. Make it a habit to express gratitude. With a grateful heart, it's difficult to feel disheartened. Keep in mind what God has done for you in the past to give you hope in the Lord.

What is it today that is enticing you to be discouraged? Are you having trouble believing that God will use what appears to be a negative situation for good (Romans 8:28)?

Then, rather than pouting or shrinking, it's time to fight. Consider discouragement as a choking of your faith. It's not the time to plop down in front of the television with a platter of comfort food to medicate your sadness when you're choking. So that you can breathe, you must dislodge the impediment. You must battle for your life. You may need someone to administer spiritually the Heimlich maneuver to you.

Get some faith-fueled courage by going out and getting some encouragement. Don't let pessimism suffocate you. Believing promises helps to dislodge it. God gave us the Scripture so that "we would have hope through the encouragement of the Scriptures" (Romans 15:4). It contains incredible statements such as:

Who will be able to separate us from Christ's love? Will affliction, or difficulty, or oppression, or hunger, or nakedness, or peril, or sword, or famine, or famine, or famine, or famine, or famine, or famine, or famine, ... No, by him who loved us, we are more than conquerors in all of these things. (Rom. 8:35; 37)

Don't let what you see control your emotions. Allow Jesus' promises to dominate your life.

I have told you these things, so that in Me you may have [perfect] peace. In the world you have tribulation and distress and suffering, but be courageous [be confident, be undaunted, be filled with joy]; I have overcome the world." [My conquest is accomplished, My victory abiding.] (John 16:33 AMP).

In the name of Jesus, fight discouragement. Life is spiritual, and there is a spirit of discouragement that we can overcome by calling on Jesus' name.

"Be sober, be cautious," (*1 Peter 5:8-9*) warns, *"for your opponent the devil goes around like a roaring lion, seeking whom he may devour." Resist him, firm in your faith, knowing that your brotherhood in the world is going through the same things you are."*

Let's look at some of Haggai's lectures on discouragement in the Bible as a good starting point.

As for the promise which I made with you when you came out of Egypt, My Spirit stands [firm and immovable] and continues with you; do not fear!' (Haggai 2:5 AMP).

The book of Haggai in the Old Testament has a lot to teach us about dealing with disappointment. These teachings are especially important for social workers, community organizers, fundraisers, instructors, legal advisers, volunteers, and even funders who are discouraged in their efforts to assist the needy.

The Jews attempting to restore the temple in Jerusalem in the book of Haggai went from energetic, well-resourced, and effective to depressed and defeated in a matter of weeks. Discouragement is depicted in real-time in this book.

We are all familiar with the feeling of discouragement, but I'd want to look at three things Haggai teaches us about it.

1. **Discouragement has a spiritual component.** Three times in the text, God is said to have fired up the spirits of the temple builders when they are encouraged and working hard (1:4). God tells the people three times to take courage when they are dejected (2:4). Why? They had lost their will to live. Discouragement is exactly that.

   Encouragement on the other hand will manifest the spirit of God as a help or reminder. "My Spirit is living in your midst," God reminds the weary laborers (2:5). Yet, when we support one another, we frequently concentrate almost entirely on the human spirit. "Take a gander at all the individuals you're helping, all the money you've raised, all the goals you've set!" we exclaim. We need to build on people's spiritual connections as well, using God's instruments of the bible and prayer in our encouragement ministry.

2. **Discouragement is obsessed with how things appear on the outside.** The temple architects understood their new structure would pale in comparison to Solomon's magnificent structure (2:3). But here's the real jewel of Haggai: despite the temple's diminutive size on the outside, God promises that "the latter grandeur of this house will be greater than the earlier" (2:9). God's presence would dwell in the temple in a greater way than Solomon's temple, making up for its lack of appearance.

   What was strange is that the Old Testament never mentions God moving in. God eventually appears in this temple when Jesus appears, and He says that even this temple refers to another one — Himself (John 2:13-22). Many on the outside will be disappointed by Jesus' role as the Final Temple, but He is God in the flesh (1:14).

   Don't get caught up in what seems on the surface, in what you can judge by what people notice, in your work. Look for God's work in hearts, motivations, and structures, as well as the complexity of His larger intentions that you might not notice at first.

3. **God fills in the blanks in our lives that discourage us.** It appears that when the temple workers were frustrated, they quit working as well (2:4). God begins working on them at this point. God acts as a kind of foreman in Haggai's book. The foreman on a building site may not comprehend the entire design or where his or her component fits in, but the employees do.

   The same should go for us when we're frustrated that our efforts are yielding little or no results, when we're unemployed, or when we're disheartened for no obvious cause. You may not see how everything in your life — the highs and lows, the disappointments, and unwelcome stops — fits into God's plan for your life and work, even though he does. When your job is at its most difficult, pay special attention to God's renovation work on you.

Did you even know that you're referenced in Haggai if you're a Christian? "I will shake all nations, and all nations' treasures will come in, and I will fill this home with glory, says the Lord of hosts," God says (2:7). God miraculously shares His glory with humans so that they might return it to Him. What's the result? "And in this location, declares the Lord of Hosts, I will grant peace" (2:9).

Shalom — full-orbed flourishing for all of God's creation — is the word for peace here. If that's what you're looking for, you've got every reason to "take courage... and work; for I am with you," as the Lord proclaims (2:4).

Five Ways to Avoid Getting Overwhelmed by Discouragement
Even the strongest and greatest of people can experience discouragement. When you start feeling the black cloud of discouragement engulfing you, follow the five steps listed below.

- **Be Truthful**. It's pointless to act as if you don't feel what you're feeling. You can't do anything about a negative sensation until you acknowledge it. A strong Christian isn't someone who never feels bad. It's someone who knows what to do with them once they've arrived and how to deal with it spiritually.

- **Look After Your Body.** Your intellect, emotions, and willpower are all diminished when your body isn't performing properly. I appreciate how God took care of Elijah's body first—before dealing with anything else—and fed him with birds. Life's circumstances might deplete us at times, and we need to pause, stop doing, and simply rest and rejuvenate.

- **Give Heed to Your Inner Being.** As Christians, we must learn to think genuinely *(Philippians 4:8)* and submit all thinking to Christ's obedience. *(2 Corinthians 10:5)*.

We are all trying to make sense of what is going on in our lives. We strive to understand why they occur and what they mean. It is critical that we give heed to the tales we tell ourselves about ourselves, others, God, or a certain circumstance, and whether those narratives are true. For example, most of what Elijah was saying to himself when he grew disheartened was untrue, but it added to his unhappiness because he believed it *(1 Kings 19)*.

Jeremiah had likewise taught himself untrue things about God, he lost hope because his mind trusted his interpretation of truth rather than God's. Read the third chapter of Lamentations. Jeremiah begins to have a change of heart and thought in verse 21. "This is what I recall, therefore I have hope," he says. Even while his circumstances remained the same, as his thoughts changed, so did his bad emotions.

- **Develop the Ability to Simultaneously "View" Life Via Two perspectives.** Whenever the apostle Paul teaches us to be converted by the refreshing of our minds *(Romans 12:2)*, he is implying that our minds need to be retrained to think in new ways. Learning to see both the temporary (life is hard) and the eternal (God has a purpose here) at the same time is a part of this training.

When Paul says he is pressed on all sides, puzzled, harassed, and struck down, he is speaking honestly about his temporary agony. Despite everything, he was not crushed, despondent, abandoned, or ruined. What's to stop you? Because he learned to keep his spiritual eyes firmly fixed on the everlasting view. *"As a result, we do not lose heart,"* he explains. As a result, we direct our gaze on the unseen rather than the visible. *"What is seen is fleeting, but what is unseen endures forever" (2 Corinthians 4:8–18).*

Paul rarely downplayed the transitory anguish, but he refused to be discouraged because he knew God was at work. For another example, see *(Philippians 1:12–14.)*

- **Close Your Eyes and Focus on God.** The truth is that life is difficult, that people disappoint and harm us, and that we do not always comprehend God and His methods. *"For my thoughts are not your thoughts, neither are your ways my ways." Declares the Lord. "As the heavens are higher than the earth, so are my ways. Isaiah 55:* Life's difficulties might become unbearable if we don't have a close, trusting relationship with God. *"I would have despaired unless I had believed I would see God in the land of the living,"* the psalmist said (Psalm 27).

One last point to consider. The greatest method to get rid of a bad sensation is to replace it with a good one. *"In everything give thanks, because this is God's will,"* the Bible says in *(1 Thessalonians 5:18).* Gratitude is a potent antidote to depression. We may not be able to thank God for the unpleasant circumstance we are in, but we may learn to look for things to be glad for while we are there.

CHAPTER FIVE

Intentionally work as the Ant works. (Can work unsupervised)

None of us can buy wisdom therefore it is not for sale. The wisdom of ants is brought into sharp focus: It is a priceless human trait, but when a man is too lazy to reason with himself in life, man will be less sensitive and unreasonable towards the lessons the ants can teach him.

These insects are little, yet they are incredibly wise, and they may awe you to no end. The richest and greatest man who ever lived, King Solomon, emphasized the wisdom of ants, instructing us to go to the ants and learn their methods.

Go to the ant, O lazy one; Observe her ways and be wise, Which, having no chief, Overseer or ruler, She prepares her food in the summer And brings in her provisions [of food for the winter] in the harvest. (Proverbs 6:6-8).

Most of us today are following celebrities and influential individuals around the world to learn their methods, while the Scripture instructs us to seek out the ants for wisdom. In this chapter, I want to show you how ants organize themselves and plan for the future by applying their intelligence. It takes discernment to know what season they're in. Like ants, people should ask, know, or discern their season of life. Ants understand the importance of organization diligence and not being slothful. Whatever they put their hands to do, they give it their best: like the ant, we too need to know how to work and not require supervision to accomplish specific goals.

Never allow difficulty to make you give up. You'll be surprised at what you can accomplish!

You and I should likewise go over to the ants and understand their ways, considering there is nothing more valuable than free wisdom from the ants. You can study ants in the woods, your backyard, kitchen, garden, or wherever else you think you could find them, and learn how they coordinate together, advance, transfer items, and construct Ant homes. It can take months to completely comprehend their methods.

Have you ever seen an ant colony in action? Perhaps you have a mental image of the person or group of people that "work like ants."

What Is the Scriptural Take on Ants' Wisdom?

According to the Holy scriptures, Ants: they are weak, but they store up their food in the summer. (Proverbs 30:25 GNT).

If one pays close attention, one'll notice that the ants advance in two ways (towards the inside and outwardly) and that they walk in lines to carry food items, which could include edible fragments left by people, little bone fragments of fish, as well as other pieces. The most astounding thing is how they figure out that it's summer and that they should stock up on food in preparation for autumn or wet weather. Nobody informs them, yet their intelligence allows them to do so.

Countless people, including myself and scholars, have been fascinated by the knowledge of ants. Those who can count the number of eggs they have and sort them by age. As the ants advance in search of food, they leave traces for their comrades to follow to locate the food source and return.

Should anyone damage their course or direction, they will immediately discover that there is a breakdown and will change course to construct a new way. No one tells them what to do. These ants are also highly responsive to the smell of the food, allowing them to determine where food is located within a specified interval.

Despite the lack of a leadership structure, the ants are extremely organized, value themselves, sacrificing for each other, and are willing to fight and die for each other. Because there is no such thing as selfishness between them. They collaborate and reap the benefits of their efforts jointly. People have a hard time comprehending ants' knowledge. Despite their small bodies, they are capable of carrying food ten times their weight.

I have been watching those creatures. It's fascinating to track where they are traveling from and to, and they appear to exchange greetings as they march and pass each other. They can transport dead insects such as roaches, spiders, scorpions, as well as other dead insects into underground storerooms when they work together.

I was recently reading the Scriptural Book of Job, and thus to my astonishment, I discovered that God had taken away the insight of the peacock as well as the ostrich and the powerful lesson in it. Wow such a magnificent sweet Lord! He gifted the peacock exquisite wings, and yet she does not mind treading on her offspring and murdering them because she lacks wisdom and understanding. When you lack wisdom and understanding you run the risk of forfeiting your future.

"She treats her young cruelly, as if they were not hers; Though her labor is in vain because she is unconcerned [for the safety of her brood], For God has made her forget wisdom, and has not given her a share of understanding". (Job 39:16-17 AMP).

In several biblical scriptures you can see where Gods wisdom is connected with creation. The Almighty God, who created all creatures, is well familiar with their skills, motivations, comprehension, and all other aspects of their personalities. He granted the horse the courage to charge into combat without fear of bows and arrows, spears, bullets, and perhaps other war weaponry.

Ants' Wise Advice as to Living Intentionally

Furthermore, let us be educated about Ants' teachings or Scripture teachings for Ants. God is wisdom, in the sense that He is the fountain of knowledge; He is also the one who bestows wisdom on those who deserve it and withholds it from those who do not. *The fear of the Lord is the beginning of wisdom, And the knowledge of the Holy One is understanding (Proverbs 28:28 NKJV)*. This in known to every believer.

As a result, if you fear the Lord, you are wise or full of wisdom by default. This suggests that ants are one of the wisest organisms on the planet, as they fear the Lord. They use moonlight and sunlight for navigation in their nests, according to scientists. As a result, they'd have no trouble moving around.

1. **The Ants Intentionally Care for One Another.** The next ant teaching, or ants' scripture learning experience, is about how they look after one another intentionally (Philippians 2:4). We can learn from the ants' desire for each other's success by giving support to those in need. As you desire good things for your neighbor, good and nice things will undoubtedly come to you as well.

2. **The Ants Intentionally Love One Another.** The next Holy book teaching about the ant is again how they demonstrate love with intent by putting down their lives for each other. They are always willing to die for one another,

according to the Bible, and there is no greater love than laying down one's life for one's friends (John 15:13).

3. **The Ants Intentionally Invest for the Future.** I want everyone to pay attention to the next ant's teaching, which is about how they invest in the future. They are clever enough just to recognize that there will come a moment when it will be challenging for them to obtain food or wander in search of food, erecting ant towns, and so on, so they prepare by storing food in their chamber. They would not be in any danger in the future if cold or wet seasons arrived.

Therefore, we must understand that it is wise to utilize our current assets and abilities into something beneficial to feel comfortable in the future; we should not wait for a disaster to strike before taking action. We can plan for the future by getting various insurances, not spending everything we earn, real estate investments., We also should plan ahead of time to be progressive.

4. **The Ants Intentionally Trust Each Other.** Another important lesson humans may learn from these little organisms is the importance of trust. They are not deceitful.

The worker ants or scouts can teach us a valuable life lesson. These ants are on their way to get food. They leave behind particular molecules (pheromones) to assist them to find their way home as they go further away (nest).

Ants inform the ant colony about the food source. They go out in search of food, trusting the scouts.

May we all gain knowledge to be honest people from the ants, which will aid in the development of our varied societies.

Let us quickly also study ANTS's acronyms (T Bar M Camps & Retreats March 2014)!

A – Attitude of Initiative: Ants don't require orders from a commander to get started. If you sense a need and believe you can meet it, go for it! The most difficult part of hard work is getting started...jump in both feet!

N – Nature of Integrity: Ants are self-disciplined workers who do not require external oversight to keep them on track. Integrity is a personal decision that each of us can make... Will you choose to do the right thing?

T – Thirst for Industry: Ants put in a lot of effort and will rebuild their anthill if it is destroyed. Seeing glitches and challenges as chances is a certain method to rev up your engine and keep you on track to achieve your objectives!

S – Source of Insight: In the summer, ants stockpile food. We are called to run this course of life with all of our might, even when things are going well. We are never asked to rest on our laurels and watch life pass us by. If things are going well right now, start constructing your storehouses for later...or better yet, go help a neighbor!

What does the ant acronym teach us about the intentional life?

Ants are the epitome of self-motivated individuals. They aren't restricted by their size, lack of resources, or geographical location. They don't make excuses and go right to work. They don't need to be whipped into moving, doing their jobs, or cooperating. They simply work with the intent of achieving their set goals.

This same ant's teaching seems to be astonishing, and we living beings ought to learn from it and fulfill all of our obligations.

We have been provided with a lot of gifts and abilities that the Lord wants us to put to good use! Please don't throw them out. In all we undertake, let us be willing to **GO HARD BY LIVING THE INTENTIONAL LIFE.**

Ultimately, ant teachings teach us that we should start sharing what we do have with anybody who is entitled to the fruits of our effort.

If we are going to share something amongst ourselves, we must avoid cheating. The ants do not discriminate when it comes to sharing the food stored in their colony. They have banded together to defend their path, they live purposefully.

CHAPTER SIX

Embrace the Good life, by embracing the God Life

"This is what the Lord, your Redeemer, the Holy One of Israel says, "I am the Lord your God, who teaches you to profit (benefit), Who leads you in the way that you should go". (Isaiah 48:17).

This Scripture holds truth and teaches that anything you think is valuable should be your uttermost investment priority.

Some investments can appear risky and get profitable when you invest at the right time in the right thing. Investments are necessary for gain or increase: living life intentionally also entails you intentionally looking for the best return on your every investment. You can never go wrong when you invest in yourself.

Embracing the good life entails embracing the God life. Understand that you must not only "invest in yourself but invest yourself." It's a small price to pay that will yield a great return. God understood the power of investment when he invested himself by incorporating himself in the human world and becoming the answer to problems. He invested his only begotten son to yield the return of many sons.

Embracing the good life by Embracing the God life means understanding that investments can sometimes stretch you to a place of discomfort.

Embracing the good life by embracing the God life is to consistently conduct yourself with God-like communication. Understanding and utilizing the power of your words; what you say to yourself and about your circumstances can affect your atmosphere or outcomes. So, it must be infused with God's word.

"God means what he says. What he says goes. His powerful Word is sharp as a surgeon's scalpel, cutting through everything, whether doubt or defense, laying us open to listen and obey. Nothing and no one can resist God's Word. We can't get away from it—no matter what". (Hebrews 4:12-13 MSG).

So, heed intentionally. *(Proverbs 18:21AMP) Death and life are in the power of the tongue, and those who love it and indulge it will eat its fruit and bear the consequences of their words.*

Whether you like it or not the words you speak will create your world. The Greek word for word is "Sperma" which means that words have the ability to impregnate possibilities just like a natural pregnancy of a woman with a child. There'll come a time when that word will produce or bring forth fruit or harvest. Embracing the good life by embracing the God life means to live intentionally; to always sow purposely and not accidentally. Every word written by the patriarchs and inspired by the Holy Spirit is a purposeful word that is meant to bring forth the harvest God meant.

Don't quit on your God Given Purpose. It had to be grueling and even heartbreaking for Jesus to get from Gethsemane to Golgotha, we too must pass certain tests where we just don't throw in the towel! If we get to the cross, and died to our carnal challenges, we will ultimately elevate to our next level. On the third day, Jesus not only was raised from the dead but he then qualified for elevation. Quit or qualify that is the question!

See six reasons why you should embrace God's plan for your life.

In this chapter, we will explore six reasons that clearly explain why you should embrace God's Purpose for Your Life. This is an excerpt from the Shortform book guide by Rick Warren's "Purpose Driven Life".

1. **It Isn't All About You.** The Bible reveals that the significance of your life isn't about you. Everything in your life is connected to God: your beginnings, meaning, identity, and purpose. It isn't about achieving your goals in life. It's all about doing God's will.

   This is an eternal truth since it is God's Word. This should be the foundation of your existence, not guesswork about what you or others believe to be the truth.

   Many people (and self-help books) mistakenly believe that "success" is the true meaning of life yet being successful by world standards and fulfilling your mission are not synonymous. You may be missing out on the bigger purpose of your time on earth if you pursue an imagined truth rather than everlasting realities. By guessing reality, you won't be able to discover your identity and meaning. Only by following God and accepting God's purpose for your life can you discover the ultimate meaning of your life.

2. **There's a reason you're here.** You weren't made at random; God imagined and created you long before you were born. Every part of you and your life has a purpose, such as:

   Your ethnicity, physical characteristics, abilities, and personality. Where you were born and where you lived are both important factors. When you were born and when you will die are both important dates in your life. Your parents' influence on your life and the quality of their parenting. Accept God's plan for your life and give thanks.

Your existence is a wonderful gift. God does not require company because he is the essence of love and a part of the Trinity's perfect friendship. He created you just to express his love. God didn't stop there; he loves and appreciates us above all of his other creations. He constructed a beautiful home for us to demonstrate this.

Biologists and scientists have uncovered numerous ways in which the planet is perfectly suited to human requirements. According to some scientists, the only answer is that the universe was created particularly to support human life.

It's impossible not to be overwhelmed by an appreciation for all of God's hard work and love in your life. You'll never be able to repay him for everything he's done for you, but you may show your appreciation by living your life as God intended.

3. **Purpose-driven behavior promotes peace.** External causes such as issues or pressure, emotional elements such as anxiety or fear, or moral considerations such as values and beliefs all play a role in how people live their lives. You won't be able to find tranquility in your life if you're driven by the incorrect motivators. Unfortunately, five typical "wrong" motivators motivate a lot of people:

- **Guilt:** You're controlled by your past when you're motivated by guilt, and you often destroy your achievement without recognizing it. Your entire life revolves around avoiding feelings of guilt or regret.

- **Resentment**: Resentment motivates you to cling to wrongdoings and allow them to continue to damage you, rather than forgiving and letting go. This will either force you to withdraw and internalize your anger, or it will cause you to lash out and disseminate your anger, both of which will harm your relationships.

- **Fear:** Fear can stem from worry, trauma, perfectionism, or controlling parents, among other things— when you're driven by fear, you spend your life maintaining the status quo and avoiding any risk of failure. This is a huge impediment because it is through attempting new things and failing that you learn and overcome your worries.

- **Materialism:** If you're motivated by materialism, you'll put riches and material belongings at the center of your life, frequently in the hopes of making you happier, more important, and more secure. Wealth, on the other hand, will not make you feel happier or more significant; only a strong, positive sense of self-worth can achieve that. Furthermore, money is never guaranteed. You can easily lose all of your wealth in an instant for a variety of reasons.

- **The need for approval:** When you're driven by a desire for approval, you're concerned about what others might think of you and your decisions, and you believe that doing what others want would keep you from being judged. This allows you to delegate control of your life to others, such as friends, parents, or your spouse.

4. **There's More to Life Than This:** You're not a permanent resident of the planet; you're only a tourist passing through. Many Christians, on the other hand, appear to feel that their true homes and lives are here on earth. It's critical to remember that the genuine "you" exists in eternity, where you came from, and will return one day. There is no precise description of what awaits you in eternity or what it will look like—it is much beyond human comprehension. However, you can learn about the splendors of God's kingdom and how you might be rewarded for your loyalty by turning to the Bible:

You'll be reunited with your long-lost loved ones. You'll be free of any agony or suffering you've endured on this planet. For the rest of your life, you'll experience eternal joy and peace!

Why It's Vital to Consider Death More.
Several people are afraid of death or perceive it as gloom or unjust. You might believe this is due to a yearning for immortality—for your life on Earth to extend indefinitely. It's because God intended for us to have eternal life. We have a notion that death is "unfair" or "unnatural" because of our intrinsic awareness of endless living.

The knowledge of eternal life, on the other hand, should make death less terrible and morbid to contemplate. In fact, you should think about death and eternity more often as it is the end and the beginning.

How Eternal Thoughts Reduce Stress.
How Eternal Thoughts Reduce Stress: you have nothing to be concerned about or unsure about because you already know what will happen next.

Getting comfortable with the concept of eternity and pondering on it regularly has a good impact on every element of your life.

- It demonstrates how insignificant small, ordinary worries are. You can rapidly move on from them and concentrate on more eternal aims and concerns.

- Thinking about what matters and what doesn't in eternity can help you decide how to respond to certain problems and situations.

- You understand that any harm or suffering that may occur is merely transitory, even if it is frightening or terrible.

- Instead of squandering your money and time on transient or sinful pleasures, you invest them in more gratifying and smart ways.

- You prioritize what's genuinely valuable—you recognize that money and success won't last forever, so you concentrate on your character and relationships.

5. **Life Is Both a Test and a Responsibility:** "How do I envision my life?" you might wonder. Your reaction, to use a life metaphor, tells everything about you: what matters to you, what you expect from life, how you view your circumstances, your goals, and so on.

    If you say, "My life is a whirlwind," you're probably thinking of life as rapid and complicated, and you don't feel like you're completely appreciating things as they pass you by. If you say, "Life is a war," you might believe that life is difficult and full of struggles and that there is a method to "win" or "lose" it.

    Everything in your life is influenced by how you view it: your relationships, how you spend your time or money, your values, your ambitions, and so on. Accepting God's plan for your life allows you to redefine your perspective on life: the Bible says that life is both a test and a responsibility.

    a. **Life Is a Test**
    God will bring conflicts, troubles, changes, and success into your path throughout your life to test you. These scenarios are designed to test your faith, character, love, and loyalty, among other things.

You can't predict how God will put you to the test, but catastrophes, unanswered prayers, undeserved hurt, and dramatic changes are all examples of how people are tested. God allows these challenges in order to both expose undeveloped areas in your life and teach the lesson in it.

Even if you can't feel God, He's still right there.
When you can't feel God's presence, God is especially interested in how you respond. In two situations, God appears to be absent:

- **Challenging conditions:** When things are going well for you, it's simple to experience God's presence. When things go tough, it's much more difficult to feel him—as it's as if he's forgotten or abandoned you. The genuine test of faith is continuing to believe God and trust him in the face of enormous difficulties.

- **Small, moments of insignificance**: In enormous, significant events and situations, it's simple to sense God. It's far more difficult to recognize that he's involved in everything, no matter how minor or insignificant. Knowing that everything in your life has been placed there indicates that every moment of your life is significant and adds to your character development.

b. **Life entails a certain amount of responsibility.**
God is the true owner of everything on earth since he created it, but he entrusted all of his gifts to you during your time here as a sign of his love.

These gifts can take many forms, including your unique talents, the natural environment, your relationships, and the experiences you encounter, among others. You're responsible for looking after all God has given you to the best of your ability. This is known as stewardship, and it is some of the most important work you will ever do since it demonstrates your level of accountability. God will assess each of the things he bestowed upon you at the end of your life to see how effectively you cared for and utilized them. If he finds you to be a good steward of his gifts, you'll be rewarded with Godly benefits: God's approval, vital and intriguing eternal responsibilities, and celebration.

6. **Everything is done in the name of God and for the sake of God:** God created the entire creation to show his essence, existence, strength, and love. Everything in your environment is a reflection of his majesty.

Consider the human body's incredible and faultless design, as well as microscopic forms of life and seasons, to name a few examples.

Aside from the gifts he's given us, God has revealed his splendor in a variety of stunning ways throughout history, including giving His only begotten son, Jesus, and allowing him to die for our sins, appearing to Moses as a burning bush, and giving him the Ten Commandments. Giving angels charge over us to keep us in all our ways. We can't possibly add to God's splendor because it is the most powerful, brilliant, and complete thing in the universe.

Instead, we reveal God's splendor as a way of expressing our thanks for what he has given us. Every time one of God's creatures accomplishes the goal He set for it; He reveals his splendor. Humans were given five tasks by Him:

- Worship
- Selflessness
- Spiritual growth
- Your kingdom assignment

- Your mission is to express your thankfulness to God and succeed in revealing his glory by completing God's plan for your life.

CHAPTER SEVEN

Avoiding Toxic Relationships. Lessons from Samson

Like a city that is broken down and without walls [leaving it unprotected] Is a man who has no self-control over his spirit [and sets himself up for trouble]. (Proverbs 25:28 AMP).

Judges 16:1-21 (AMP).
1 Then Samson went to Gaza and saw a prostitute there, and went in to her. 2 The Gazites were told, "Samson has come here." So they surrounded the place and waited all night at the gate of the city to ambush him. They kept quiet all night, saying, "In the morning, when it is light, we will kill him." 3 But Samson lay [resting] until midnight, then at midnight he got up and took hold of the doors of the city gate and the two door-posts, and pulled them up, [security] bar and all, and he put them on his shoulders and carried them up to the top of the hill which is opposite Hebron. 4 After this he fell in love with a [Philistine] woman [living] in the Valley of Sorek, whose name was Delilah. 5 So the [five] lords (governors) of the Philistines came to her and said to her, "Persuade him, and see where his great strength lies and [find out] how we may overpower him so that we may bind him to subdue him. And each of us will give you eleven hundred pieces of silver." 6 So Delilah said to Samson, "Please tell me where your great strength lies and with what you may be bound and subdued." 7 Samson said to her, "If they bind me with seven fresh cords ([a]tendons) that have not been dried, then I will be weak and be like any [other] man." 8 Then the Philistine lords brought her seven fresh cords that had not been dried, and she bound him with them. 9 Now she had men lying in ambush in an inner room. And she said to him, "The Philistines are upon you, Samson!" And he broke the cords as a [b]string of tow breaks when it touches fire. So [the secret of] his strength was not discovered. 10 Then Delilah said to Samson, "See now, you have mocked me and told me lies; now please tell me [truthfully] how you may be

bound." 11 He said to her, *"If they bind me tightly with new ropes that have not been used, then I will become weak and be like any [other] man." 12 So Delilah took new ropes and bound him with them and said to him, "The Philistines are upon you, Samson!" And the men lying in ambush were in the inner room. But he snapped the ropes off his arms like [sewing] thread.*
13 Then Delilah said to Samson, "Until now you have mocked me and told me lies; tell me [truthfully] with what you may be bound." And he said to her, "If you weave the seven braids of my hair with the web [c][and fasten it with a pin, then I will become weak and be like any other man." 14 So while he slept, Delilah took the seven locks (braids) of his hair and wove them into the web]. And she fastened it with the pin [of the loom] and said to him, "The Philistines are upon you, Samson!" And he awoke from his sleep and pulled out the pin of the [weaver's] loom and the web.

Delilah Extracts His Secret

15 Then she said to him, "How can you say, 'I love you,' when your heart is not with me? You have mocked me these three times and have not told me where your great strength lies." 16 When she pressured him day after day with her words and pleaded with him, he was annoyed to death. 17 Then [finally] he told her everything that was in his heart and said to her, "A razor has never been used on my head, for I have been a Nazirite to God from my mother's womb. If I am shaved, then my strength will leave me, and I will become weak and be like any [other] man." 18 Then Delilah realized that he had told her everything in his heart, so she sent and called for the Philistine lords, saying, "Come up this once, because he has told me everything in his heart." Then the Philistine lords came up to her and brought the money [they had promised] in their hands. 19 She made Samson sleep on her knees, and she called a man and had him shave off the seven braids of his head. Then she began to abuse Samson, and his strength left him. 20 She said, "The Philistines are upon you, Samson!" And he awoke from his sleep and said, "I will go out as I have time after time and shake myself free." For Samson did not know that the Lord had departed from him. 21 Then the Philistines seized him and gouged out his eyes; and they brought him down to Gaza and bound him with [two] bronze chains; and he was forced to be a grinder [of grain into flour at the mill] in the prison.

Looking at Samson. Samson was to be a Nazarite unto God all the days of his life and this charge was given before he was conceived. The Nazarite vow is one where you do not drink any wine or similar drink, you don't touch or eat anything unclean nor should your hair and/ or beard be cut.

The Nazarite vow can be for a specific amount of time or a lifetime. His was a lifetime. When you look at the requirements to fulfill the vow, you see it means a lifetime of self-control and discipline (no wine), a lifetime of consecration and holiness (no unclean things), and a lifetime of nonconformity to worldly ways (no hair-cutting). Yet we see that Samson though graced with physical strength, was weak and careless in character and spiritual strength. His first mistake, seeking to marry and start a family with a philistine woman.

This decision was based on how pleasurable she was to the eyes. Though his parents tried to give him wise counsel, he sought to follow his lust for the eyes. Toxic people may not exhibit outright toxic behaviors right away but if it's in the heart eventually you will see it in their actions.

Next, we see *(Isaiah 30:12–13) play*. *"Wherefore thus sauté the Holy One of Israel, because ye despise the word and trust in oppression and perverseness and stay there on: Therefore, thus iniquity shall be to you like a breach ready to fall a budge in a high wall. Whose breaking comes suddenly, in an instant"*.

Samson's now philistine wife instead of telling her husband of the threat from the philistines if she doesn't give up his secret, she pressures her husband for an answer to a riddle. Toxic people are people who only think of themselves.

Samson falls into deeper darkness after the murder of his wife and father-in- law and seeks comfort in his flesh (lust of the flesh) with a prostitute instead of seeking to have his soul restored by God. Toxic thoughts can connect us with toxic people to take toxic actions and ultimately put us in a toxic situation. For him, in a darken place, his enemies waited on a moment of opportunity.

Now we are here and Samson has traveled to Sorek which means the valley of choice. One thing stands out to me, it was a valley, and he was in a low terrain. Samson was in a place where he could have repented and not met the fate that awaited him. Instead, He falls in love with Delilah which means delicate or seductress.

This toxic woman delicately and persistently through emotional tactics convinced Samson to give up his secret to his strength. Again, toxic people only think of themselves. She sold him out for gain. And after being captured by his enemies his eyes with gauge out (causing blindness) and he was bound. Toxic people in your life have the propensity to cause you to be both spiritually blind and in bondage to your enemies.

It was only when Samson repented that he gained his spiritual sight, and spiritual and physical strength back. Destroying his enemies even unto his demise. Truth: we don't have to die with our enemies, God will make a way to escape *(1Cor 10:13)* the question is in the valley of the decision: will you decide to not only rid yourself of toxic friends and relationships but seek to repent of any toxic thoughts or actions?

Intentional and Godly relationship lesson from Samson and Delilah:

1. **Position:** To begin, it's crucial to note that Samson traveled to Gaza and encountered a prostitute. As a result, pay attention to where you're headed since that's where destiny or doom will meet you. Samson encountered this prostitute in Gaza and stayed with her for the night. It's fascinating that

he stayed the night with her; this shows me that your relationships influence whether or not you stay in the dark. It's also important to consider how you spend your time. Listen, we're supposed to be the light of the world, not the source of further darkness. Samson had a physical relationship with a prostitute, which drove him into the pits of despair. Who are the people in your life with whom you have a intimate relationship? What do you do with your time while you're not at work? Has it cast a pall over your decisions, everyday routines, and dreams? Then you should reconsider your stance and live intentionally.

2. **Access:** Because of Samson's posture, his opponents could see him because he was in the dark—as they put it, "Samson is here!" His foes encircled him and waited at the gate all night for him. Once again, the issue of time is highlighted—they waited all night—he was in the dark—your relationships either attract adversaries or shield you from them. Your relationships either expose you or protect you. All the while, Samson was able to get away because of his strength. Your calling can only shield you for so long until you have to defend it. Samson's mission shielded him by providing a means of escape. Your mission will always lead you to the light, but you have the option of staying in the dark. Samson's mission allowed him to flee, but he decided to stay in the darkness. You must be intentional in proactive decision making.

3. **Attraction:** The people you find attractive are influenced by where you spend your time. Samson seemed to have spent a lot of time doing physical things, such as sleeping with a prostitute. As a result, he was drawn to Delilah and fell in love with her—yet another example of his foolish choices with women. Relationships are incredibly powerful, understand that. You must be cautious about who has access to your life; Samson granted Delilah access and, by extension, his adversaries. It's fascinating that the Bible

claims he fell in love with Delilah—have you had a Delilah in your life? Do you cultivate your flesh or your spirit, as the case may be? Is it your flesh or your spirit that he/she is appealing to? He fell in love with her because he was engrossed with his body, but she was no good for him—she was not looking out for his best interests. She turned on him in front of his foes. Have you allowed your adversaries access to you because of your relationship with that person? Because you were drawn to them in the flesh, don't be surprised if they follow the flesh's lead rather than the Spirit's:

Consider the following scenario:

i. Delilah was a shrewd businesswoman who traded Samson for silver. Her flesh was guiding her. Is that individual willing to compromise your trust for money, as she betrayed his for money? You'll notice it in their actions—how do they behave when it comes to money, for example? When it comes to money, how do they communicate? Do they have a history of betraying individuals for money? Be wary of such individuals; they can be extremely deadly. Do they follow the guidance of the spirit or the guidance of the flesh? This will also be seen in their daily activities.

ii. Delilah was self-centered, and she insisted on learning the key to Samson's incredible power and how to bind and tame him. This is self-evident—I'm astonished Samson didn't recognize the gravity of her question—anyone who cares about you will not want to damage you. Delilah was intentional in her actions but not completely informed as to how Samson might be harmed to benefit her. So, has that person harmed you on purpose and numerous occasions? Then it's very evident they don't care about you—have their behaviors demonstrated that they're selfish?

iii. Samson was blinded by sexual desire. Samson heard Delilah's query, but he didn't pay attention to the reason for it—she wanted to know how he could be chained and tamed, so she asked for the secret of his power. He was in love with her, as the Word previously stated; don't fall in love with the wrong person, as they will create an avenue for entry to your enemies. Samson became spiritually deaf as a result of his lust for Delilah. Interestingly, he lied to her because this demonstrates spiritual resistance—you can't be touched unless your spirit and flesh agree—Samson agreed with Delilah in his flesh but not in his soul. He was spiritually deaf, though, because he couldn't detect her treason and cooperative allegiance with the Philistines. Why was he so spiritually dull? Delilah announced their arrival three times, and he never asked why they arrived after he gave her the information she needed. Another red flag: have you revealed to an individual a secret that has somehow made its way out into the open? Then it's evident that they aren't looking out for your best interests.

iv. Delilah was cunning. she maintained giving the Philistines whatever Samson ordered her, then feigned to provide an escape route by alerting their presence. Be aware of such individuals; they will get you into difficulties and then claim to be the source of your remedies! Have you listened to what God has taught you about that person via their acts? This is what Delilah did to Samson, and God revealed all of her characteristics to him through her actions. When you're spiritually deaf, you're only a few steps away from spiritual blindness, and Samson was on the verge of that.

v. Delilah was a master of disguise. She was always the victim—she claimed Samson made a mockery of her even though Samson was the victim here—has someone in your life played the victim when you have suffered as a result of their problems? Then they are a Delilah, and they are cunning. Stop giving those individuals chances to betray you; Samson gave up his secret for her consolation, which she exploited against him once more. Delilah betrayed Samson once more because it was in her character, and he suffered the consequences of her betrayal. Is there a history of betrayal here—has this individual betrayed you multiple times? Then cease providing them multiple opportunities to sabotage your goal. Because, despite his enemies' failures, they kept getting closer to the source of his strength because of Delilah, this was an attack on Samson's purpose and strength—the more time you spend with toxic influences, the more exposed you leave your purpose—because, despite his enemies' failures, they kept getting closer to the source of his strength because of Delilah. That is why it is crucial to quit the relationships that God has instructed you to abandon to defend your purpose.

vi. Samson can't even hide his motivation. He told her the truth because he was misled by her nagging—and he told her everything. It is not everyone's business to know your secret, and it is not everyone's business to know your narrative. And be extremely careful who you let into your heart.

vii. Delilah betrayed Samson in two ways. First, she received the money in secret, and then she continually revealed her intentions to Samson before they completely developed in the flesh. When his braids were chopped off, he was napping on her lap. He had no idea that the sign of his strength has vanished. The more you give in to that, the Lord withdraws Himself, the less sensitive you become to God's presence, and the less insight you have into your destiny. Samson had no idea that the LORD had abandoned him, and this text has always struck a chord with me. How could he not know that the LORD had abandoned him while he was consecrated to God, I wondered? And the answer is that he was no longer in a relationship with God because he had broken the covenant by telling Delilah the secret.

viii. Physically and Spiritually Blindness. It's interesting that the enemies, the Philistines, gouged out his eyes since it represents blindness—which also indicates you get spiritually blind before you go physically blind. Before the enemies could tear out Samson's eyes, the LORD withdrew Himself from him. As a result, his spiritual awareness was taken away before it manifested in the physical realm—and this is how relationships work: they either bind you or free you.

ix. Freedom and Slavery. Samson was shackled and imprisoned, symbolizing the fact that he was once again enslaved to bondage. And that is what happens when you let Delilah into your life—it may begin with that prostitute, which is symbolic of those distraction—those companions, those vices, but if it continues, it leads to spiritual blindness and slavery. Delilah was no longer there when she had served her purpose—to destroy his life—so stop fooling yourself into thinking that whoever that person is will be there for you through thick and thin—they serve a purpose—and once they have served that purpose and given the enemy entry, they end up leaving.

Therefore, are you contemplating engaging with a Delilah? Make no mistake of such and start living a purposeful and intentional life.

The narrative of Samson and Delilah fascinates me. He'd met ladies like her before, but for some reason, he couldn't break free from the poison of that relationship, which forced him to give up a significant part of his calling.

Why do we fall prey to these types of relationships at different times in our lives? Why is it that the blindness of this ostensibly loving emotion often leads us to trust individuals who do not deserve it? What is it that prevents us from progressing and establishing independent and strong judgments about our lives, relationships, and resources?

It all boils down to your commitment and capacity to recognize all of your harmful interactions. Your lack of knowledge in this area could end up costing you a lot of money, wasted time, heartache, etc. You know you are in a poisonous connection when a friendship or relationship drains your love and zeal for God. It may have an impact on your marriage, your relationship with others, or loyalty to God's house. In other instances, the person may act like a leech, sucking your money, valuable resources, confidence, trust, or the very life out of you.

After you have narrowed down your options, concentrate on consciously removing the top two or three harmful connections from your life. It will be difficult for you to make a significant change in your relationships overnight, which is why you must prioritize the top few relationships to which you want to dedicate the most attention.

I am not sure whether its because relationship is a RE word, but most of the advice I have for you in this section starts with a RE. When you surrender to the Lord and permit Him to REalign your relationships, He will RE-do your entire life, to the point that your future will appear to be RE-designed! Consider the tips beneath, as we learn to avoid toxic relationships.

1. **Resolve:** It all starts with a determination to get yourself out of this relationship's entrapment and enticement. This could take a little time for you to arrive at this point, yet most of us stay and never decide to leave. That is why we tend to stay trapped in the muck for as long as we do. No one can ever make your decision for you, and no one should ever have to force you to finish it. You won't be able to get out of it unless you're certain that this person isn't supposed to be in your life. Therefore, seek God's insight, help and RESOLVE! And that includes the requirement to convey your intention to the

other party, whether or not you provide precise facts about why you need to end your connection with him or her.

2. **Redirect:** Learn to refocus your emotions and time investments. This is an intermediate step you must do before you begin the process of getting over your relationship. You should devote your time and effort to something more beneficial and valuable instead of this person. You must be careful not to fall into another toxic relationship, which will turn into a transient rebound friendship that will be neither useful nor beneficial. Pick up a hobby, learn something new, seek counseling or mentorship, or come up with another way to keep your mind and emotions active and productive.

3. **Remove:** You must now take steps to eliminate anything in your life that reminds you of or ties you to this individual. This could include items like gifts, photos, social media accounts, emails, text messages, clothing, or any other memoirs you share with this individual. I would even advise you to delete their contact information and block them from social media. You might be thinking, "How can this individual experience God's love if I'm so ferociously disconnected from them?" I would advise you to put your faith in God and His ways. Allow God to take care of and safeguard this person, and let Him do whatsoever He wants with their lives. You might not be able to get out of a physical commitment at a church, school, or workplace that you and your partner both attend. In these cases, I would advise you to communicate with persons in positions of authority in these organizations to help you keep safe from this individual. If this individual is in a position of administration or leadership in any of these locations, pray to the Lord to provide you with a new job or church to attend.

4. **Repair:** First you must work diligently to ensure that every fracture in your life is repaired and no gaps remain unfilled. Examine everything in your life to see whether there are any

wicked or selfish habits or inclinations that have developed as a result of your relationship with this individual. If you don't fix the hole in the wall, it'll only be a matter of time before the same individual or someone else breaks in and causes further havoc in your life. Take time to read, study, pray, and improve your grasp of the topic if you've fallen into sexual sin, for example. Then repent for all you have willingly participated in in the past. Also, surround yourself with solid, non-negotiable boundaries that no one may breach. This stage does not have to be connected to the individual you're detaching from all of the time. Changing who you are as a person will help you avoid bad and unholy relationships in your life! So, yes, fix your life by expanding, evolving, and changing it regularly!

5. **Replace:** You will undoubtedly have low and lonely moments throughout your life, and you may be tempted to replace this individual with someone else. You could be making a very grave mistake at this point. If you are not discerning at this point, you may have gotten rid of one toxic relationship just to fall into an even worse trap. You might also be enticed to re-enter the same relationship from which you just emerged. Please keep in mind that Jesus is the only one who is worthy of taking the throne of your heart and ruling over you. Nobody else in your life is deserving of that spot. You are not required to please or gain approval from others. So, before you fall in love with someone else, make sure you grow in your love for and desire for Jesus. People will be less able to manipulate, persecute, or hurt you the more you give Jesus the place and authority of control in your life. I've read numerous accounts of martyred saints who appear to be unaffected by their agony and sacrifice. The Lord rules and reigns over them, and this is their secret.

6. **Restore:** You've arrived at a point in your life when Jesus sits atop your life's throne, and you're ready to begin developing loving and trusted connections. Allow the Holy

Spirit to direct you to the right people, at the right time, and with the appropriate viewpoints. Allow him to restore your relationships in your life. It's not for you to live isolated and shut away on some mountain when God wants to prune and purify your relationships. He will lead you back into a season of fertile and growing connections after he's restored your priorities. In every Christian's life, the slogan of heaven is restoration. Whatever the adversary has taken from you, destroyed around you, and murdered inside you, God is capable of resurrecting and bringing beauty from the ashes. It may not appear to be the same as your prior relationships, but God's choice for you will prove to be the best and most beautiful alternative for you in the end.

7. **Refill:** You're now walking and living in the newness that God has given you in your relationships, remember to take time away from everyone and everything to fill and fuel yourself with God's love. One of the main reasons we get tired of people around us and are sometimes taken for granted or manipulated by them is because our care and regard for them are usually confined to a natural, human, emotional, and soulish level. It becomes simpler to resist temptation when we upgrade ourselves to think, feel, love, and care as God does. Then this will come naturally to you not to allow yourself to be influenced or controlled by others. Because now the love of Christ will bind you and govern all of your thoughts, actions, and habits. If you want to avoid toxic friendships in the future, you must practice abiding in God's love, getting a fresh refill of God, and a revelation of his mercy and grace over your life daily.

CHAPTER EIGHT

Let Go and Let God restore the dreamer in you

"Trust in and rely confidently on the Lord with all your heart and do not rely on your insight or understanding." (Proverbs 3:5 AMP)

What does it mean to let go and let God? What does it mean to give it to God? Most people believe it entails giving up one's hopes, objectives, and comfort, but this is not the case. Giving it to God entails releasing your ego and allowing your spirit to be directed by God, believing His path.

We are truly yielding to God when we let go and let God. We are letting go of anything we have been attempting to accomplish on our own so that God can do what only He can accomplish. Surrendering to God really means acknowledging God in all our ways. It's a way of informing God that we're too small to handle our problems on our own, that we are dependent on His Omnipotence and in doing so, it has to be truly intentional.

We give God room to exercise His strong arm in our lives when we finally let go. God's hands are strong and powerful even when ours are feeble and exhausted!

Your arm is endowed with power; your hand is strong, your right hand exalted. (Psalm 89.13 NIV).

The phrase "let go and let God" has become a popular one. When we are feeling overwhelmed, we are admonished to give

God everything. It's a happy-go-lucky expression that doesn't always have to allude to God.

If you have ever wanted the Almighty God to save you, like I have been saved, you might be pondering what it means to "let go." And what role He will play when you "allow God" to assist in restoring you?

Therefore, what does it truly mean to "let go and let God" in our lives? This is divided into two parts: our part and God's portion. We must determine what we are releasing and what we are allowing God to do.

Let's break down the phrase and examine its meaning:

Let Go - Let go of a situation, ideals, patterns, things that are impeding your progress, or things to which you are clinging too firmly. This can apply to anything that comes into your life.

Let God - Allow God to take those things and demonstrate to you that He is faithful to see you through. It's all about handing over control of your life to God.

Fundamentally, it's about giving up control and allowing God to take care of your problems and restore the dreamer in you.

It's easier said than done, but it's worth it. Oh, the joy and peace found in Christ!

How to Let Go and Let God

Let it go and I think God doesn't simply mean throwing your hand up on your business ideas, relationships, or even salvation; it does simply mean recognizing that God has a plan and an even better one for your life. There's a certain serenity that comes with it: surrendering to God's plan. It's not always easy for us to do this because we are always in survival mode—taking matters into our hands.

Proverbs 25:2 says it is the glory of God to conceal a thing but the owner of kings is to search out the matter. Handing over things to God does not mean haphazardly going through life. It basically mean leaning on God with our hopes and objectives. It means to look to the truth which is the word of God to be a lamp that guides your footsteps. It means not being persuaded by our emotions but to allow the spirit of God to direct our path. When you truly yield to God, your philosophy in life will be all things work together for your good. That even the things that caused anguish, God will turn around and use them as a blessing in the lesson of life.

You will walk confidently when certain doors have been shut in your life: it's only because God has a better door for you and the absolute fact that no man can shut a door God has opened. It means to give God your broken heart and not harbor unforgiveness. It means to not dwell on your past failures but to know that every morning there is a brand-new mercy, a fresh new start that God has made available to us to overcome obstacles that have held us back, make new friends to replace those who have walked away, be brave enough to step out of the boat (your comfort zone) that's holding you back from greatness, history-making achievements again believing that if you let go and let God, anything is possible!

In my ministry walk, I've found that if some people would let go of even physical hurts and trust the word of God, healing can effortlessly come forth.
Give God room to exercise His authority and strong arm. Give God room in your life you trust his timetables.
Fundamentally, it's about giving God ultimate control; though He has given you the ability to make choices.

It is a daily, moment-by-moment decision to let go and let God. We must learn to resign and offer it to God, just as we must with any other discipline in life. Every day, the enemy tries to fill our heads with worry, doubts, and fears.

The devil wishes for us to have no room for God in our life. To let go and let God becomes a daily practice of surrendering everything to Him.

We must trim the nasty hairs of negative ideas whenever they try to invade our space and surrender them to God right away.

Every morning, God's mercies are new, therefore whatever happened yesterday, last year, or a decade ago is utterly forgotten.

Having to carry the past shortcomings will only take up room that could be used to celebrate God's goodness, love, grace, mercy, and favor. Renewing our minds in Christ entails releasing all of the responsibilities that He died to relieve us of.

Let go and let God have your worries and fears. Let go and let God have your finances. Let go and let God have control. Let go and let God restore. Let go and let God have your future.

You can start letting go and letting God do what He does best by doing the following:

- **Start each day with prayer -** Speak to God – and give it to God. Yes, the day is packed with obligations, but take some time to chat with God first. Grasp His Hand. Declare your devotion to Him. Tell Him how grateful you are for Jesus' death on the cross. Allow the Holy Spirit to lead you on that particular day. Talk to God first before approaching anyone else. He'll help you start your day off right.

- **Start giving it to God by surrounding yourself with positive people.** You will never be able to do it on your own. You need individuals in your life who tell you the truth. You can also engage yourself with Christian music, read books, view films, and listen to podcasts to strengthen your faith and spirit. Always be on the watch for individuals and resources that you may include in your life as spiritual buffers.

- **Begin each day by giving it to God.** Do not bring your mistakes from yesterday into today's fresh start. Every morning, mentally shave off all of your worries, doubts, fears, errors, and anxieties.

- **Start each day with Scripture to give it to God.** Open your Bible and continue reading where you left off the day before. Use a Bible App on your phone. Look through your emails to see if any inspiring verses have been sent to you. The Bible is alive and well, like refreshing water for a parched spirit.

- **Commit it to God by rejuvenating your thoughts regularly.** The world will want to fill your day with anxieties, therefore you must protect your spiritual health! Surrender your troubles to God regularly. Believe and trust that God is on your side. He adores you and desires nothing but the finest for you. You can completely rest in His strength when you let go. You don't have to be concerned. The World's Creator is on your side.

How to Give It to God
It's not always simple to let go of things. We have a hard time letting go even when things are awful for us and we know they are harmful. Addiction is a good example of this. So, how do we let go and surrender it to God?

- Pray for it. Giving things to God does not imply that you make a mental note to quit doing them. You must include God.

This is best illustrated by King David. You may see him express his honest thoughts toward God via the psalms (David and others). He isn't hesitant to say what he thinks, and he isn't afraid to humbly tell it like it is.

If you need to let go of something, now is the time. Then discuss it with God. Let Him know how you're feeling about it. Inviting Him to assist you in letting go is a great way to start. Invoke pity, grace, and wisdom.

- Place it at Jesus' Feet. It's only after you've prayed it out and entered God's presence that you'll be able to see it. Now is the time to lay it all at Jesus' feet. This can be done in prayer, or you can write it down and cut it up or cross it out. It's like a declaration that it doesn't have any hold over me anymore.

Make the decisions that are best for you and your circumstances. Even if I don't write it down, I prefer to mix things up with prayer.

- Refrain from picking it back up. You will have thoughts and events that make you want to take up the exact thing you have set before the Lord.

This is something that the adversary enjoys. Keep your wits about you and be cautious. Also, master the use of your weapon! (Ephesians 6:17)

If you're attempting to overcome your fear... Begin memorizing scriptures such as; *For God did not give us a spirit of timidity or cowardice or fear, but [He has given us a spirit] of power and of love and of sound judgment and personal discipline [abilities that result in a calm, well-balanced mind and self-control]. (2 Timothy 1:7).*

As a result, whenever a frightening thought arises, combat it with God's truth.

Another method of avoiding picking something up is to rebuke the concept outright. I'll have strange thoughts that I know are an attempt by the enemy to divert me, and I'll voice them aloud. "I denounce that thinking, and in Jesus' name, I will not accept that falsehood."

You can also use your prayer language during those times if you have one.

- Acquire Accountability. It is often a good idea to communicate what's going on in your life with a Christian brother or sister. So, select a trusted buddy and tell them about the area you're attempting to give to God. Request that they hold you accountable and provide a safe environment for you to communicate it with them.

- Steps 1 through 4 should be repeated again. Though if you're having trouble following steps 1--4. Then I recommend that you go over everything again. I've done it previously with specific things, and over time it breaks down strongholds in life.

  So don't be discouraged if you tried and failed to give it to God. Return to the beginning and try again. Even if it means dismantling the stronghold brick by brick. It will weaken it and lead it to topple sooner or later. Then you'll be victorious and free in that area! Hallelujah!

The Right Way to Let God and the Wrong Way to Let God
You could be thinking now... "How can there possibly be anything wrong with letting go and letting God?"

It can, however, lead to a life of lethargy, excuses, and carelessness if pushed to its logical conclusion. We must get rid of things that are obstructing our progress, but we must not use this as an excuse to avoid doing the things that we should be doing.

Faith takes charge! James makes this clear when he talks about *faith without works is dead. (James 2:14-26)*.

Consider the illustration below;

You have been stressed out while looking for work. So, you have decided to "let go and allow God." You decide to quit looking for work and trust that if God wants you to work, He will send a job to come knocking at your door.

That's a terrible way to go about things. You would like to let go of your job-hunting anxiety and "allow" God to provide you peace and guidance on where to apply.

Do you see what I mean?

This quotation is one of my favorites. It expresses just what we require.

"A scriptural interpretation of the Christian life is 'trust God and get going,' rather than 'let go and allow God."

Our trust must continue, just be strong. Learning to trust God during a situation or event and letting Him take care of it is what we mean by letting go.

We Need to Let Go and Let God in These Areas of our Life

We try to maintain control over a variety of aspects of our lives. However, I would want to offer five extremely frequent areas where most believers stumble.

I recommend that you take them up in prayer to see if the Holy Spirit brings any of them to your attention.

i. **Your Relationships Should Be Given to God:** Relationships pervade our lives in every way. God, family, friends, marriage, church, and job are just a few of the things that come to me when I think of relationships. People are involved in many kinds of situations, both local and far. Fear, greed, pride, hurt, and wrath all make it simple to desire to control these relationships. We don't even realize we're doing it most of the time. It's a self-preservation mechanism.

It, on the other hand, prevents us from experiencing God's best for us in our relationships and informs God that we must rely on ourselves to be "secure."

ii. **Give Your Fears to God:** The fear factor will be present in most, if not all, of these domains.

As an illustration, consider the following:

Relationships: The fear that your husband or wife is cheating on you, prompting you to question him or her whenever they arrive home late from work.

Money: The fear of running out of money, drives you to work long hours, never tithe to your local church , operate with a not enough mentality.

Fear has the power to wreck your life and transform you into the god you worship. It'll put you in a cage and beat you with a stick. When fear tries to creep in, we must be vigilant and conscious of it so that we can demolish it before it can take root in our minds and hearts.

iii. **Give Your Dreams to God:** Remember Westlife's song "I have a Dream"? It expresses some reality in the fact that we all have dreams. It doesn't matter if we are a tough muscular guy in a gym or a 5-year-old ballerina twirling in front of the television. We all have fantasies! Things we would like to accomplish, become, or own.

Dreams, on the other hand, can become a stumbling barrier when they keep us from experiencing what God has in store for us right now. God will sometimes instruct us to write down a dream, such as my journeys across the world. We may realize why soon after, but we may not till we die and go to be with Jesus. That is something we must accept.

iv. **Give God control of your future.** A lot of individuals are concerned about the future (both personally and in the world). And they can lead to you making poor decisions in the present and/or attempting to exert control over things in the hope of improving your future.

God knows what lies ahead for us, and His Word promises that He has excellent things in store for us. (Jeremiah 19:11).

v. **Give God the opportunity to call you.** If you have ever sensed God calling you to a specific job, area, or group of people, this is the book for you. It's easy to become so engrossed in the call that we lose sight of the One who made the call. We can sometimes fall into the trap of relying solely on our strength to fulfill our mission. When it was always supposed to be a God-centered partnership.

Then there is running away from your call because you are afraid of it. We must surrender all of these things to God.

The Advantages of Giving it to God

What a list of rewards! GAINING is letting go and letting God! It's all for the sake of victory! It's for the sake of becoming liberated!

God takes His proper place in our life when we devote everything to Him. He is referred to as our Lord in this passage. We can put our faith in him. This will help to deepen and enhance your relationship with Him. However, things improve...

The book of *(Matthew 11:30 NLT)* says, *"For my yoke is easy to bear, and the burden I give you is light."*

When we give God our troubles, control, tension, fear, or whatever else we have, He will take it away from us and give us His yoke. This means he will sustain us, and give us rest from the things that depress, obstruct, and exhaust us.

He offers us His yoke, it says. His yoke is light and comfortable to wear. Peace, grace, and ease abound!

As a result, you can seek to overcome, control, or cling to your fear. You can also properly apply the term "let go and let God" to your life. And you will be filled with God's fullness in your life.

Job was given a twofold portion of all he'd lost, his marriage and many relationships were restored, he was given a new family, and he was able to live contentedly to a ripe old age.

God always has a plan to heal and restore, whether it's our emotions, finances, relationships, or lives. Although I don't know God's exact intentions for my future, I do know He is good, and I am confident that He is working on rebuilding areas in my life that need restoration.

God's restoration will always begin with complete surrender and faithfulness when you intentionally let go and let God restore the dreamer in you!

CHAPTER NINE

It's Your due season! Grab it and don't let go!

"To everything, there is a season, A time for every purpose under heaven:" (Ecclesiastes 3:1 NKJV).

"But they who wait for the Lord shall renew their strength; they shall mount up with wings like eagles; they shall run and not be weary; they shall walk and not faint." (Isaiah 40:31 ESV).

"Keep the faith, everything happens in due season. Don't rush your seasons. Be consistent. Be patient. Every blessing with your name on it is on the way!" Tony Gaskins

Sowing will bring a harvest. No matter what we choose to do with our lives, there are always consequences. As a result, make the conscious decision to live a life of purpose.

We all have things we are hoping for, aspirations we would like to accomplish, and problems we would like to solve: it could be seeing our family restored, losing weight, breaking an addiction, or starting our own business. However, if we don't see any progress month after month, or even year after year, it's easy to become disheartened and think: "It will never happen, this is as good as it gets, I will just learn to live with it." While it's fine to be pleased with where we are, we shouldn't lose sight of our goals. Because something hasn't happened yet doesn't imply it won't in the future. There will always be forces attempting to persuade us to stay put. You must rekindle your faith regularly. God hasn't brought you this far to abandon you; He intends to complete what He has begun in your life. You may not see how it will all come together, but God has a plan.

When you believe, the universe's Creator gets to work. Paul stated, *"And let us not grow weary of doing good, for in due season we will reap, if we do not give up". (Galatians 6:9 ESV).*

That which I sense in my spirit is that you are approaching your due season, a season in which God will manifest himself in your life; promises you have been standing on, dreams you have been praying for, in this due season, God will cause things to fall into place, making things happen that you couldn't make happen on your own. Things will alter in your favor in this due season, regardless of the troubles you have been expecting to turn around. You might have found it difficult to live an intentional life far too long and you have tried your hardest to break it time and time again with no success; the good news is, this is your due season to be free. Or maybe you have had financial difficulties and can't seem to move ahead, taking one stride forward and two steps behind. Allow these phrases to penetrate your soul: the right time has come. Promotion is on the way. Good news is on the way. Lack isn't your fate; always fighting and just scraping by isn't the end of the road. Continue to believe, expect, and honor God, and abundance will come your way. Your cup is likely to run over this due season.

These words of trust and victory pronounced over your life are occasionally needed. Words have creative power, and if you allow them to take root in your spirit, they may help you rekindle your dreams, faith, and inner potential. Your thoughts may try to persuade you not to do it; you have no idea how it will happen. That's fine; your task is to believe, to say, "Yes, God, this is for me today." I feel this is my due season." Many people nowadays suffer from depression; it's as if a gloomy cloud is following them around. They haven't been able to shake it in the past, and it appears that this will continue to be the case in the future, but the difference is that you have arrived at the right time; God is about to take you out of that pit, set your feet on a rock, and give you a new song to sing. Chains are broken in due season; depression cannot remain, and sadness must depart. You will experience a new level of excitement, happiness, and enthusiasm for life. Divine connections are heading your way in this due season; God is going to bring someone into your life who is better than you could have imagined.

Now you must agree with God throughout the day; say, "Lord, thank you for my due season." I feel that this is the season for me to become healthy and whole. This is the season I am going to meet the people I have always wanted to meet. This is the season for me to advance in my work, to reach a new level in my destiny." You may be confronting a situation that you have been praying about for a long time but that doesn't appear to be going away; you could easily become disheartened, accept it, and think, "I will never get healthy, my child will never straighten up, my business will never make it." No, you must prepare; you are approaching the end of that season. Things are going to alter in your favor in an unexpected, out-of-the-ordinary way. God understands how to bring you consumers, and new clients, and make you stand out in that slow-moving industry that doesn't seem to be going anywhere. God can provide you with creative thoughts, insight, and inspiration. He's known as Jehovah-Jireh, the Lord our Provider, and a single stroke of His hand can put you 50 years ahead of schedule.

Now keep believing and expecting good things to happen; don't become bored of doing the right thing. In other words, don't start whining about how things aren't working out or how they will never get better; keep your faith. Turn it around when you are inclined to be discouraged: "Lord, I want to thank you that this is my due season." This is my season to see growth, this is my season to have the baby I have always wanted, this is my season to be rid of chronic pain, to have breakthroughs in my life." This is what a lady in the Bible did: "*A woman [in the crowd] had [suffered from] a hemorrhage for twelve years, and had endured much [suffering] at the hands of many physicians.*

She had spent all that she had and was not helped at all, but instead had become worse". (Mark 5:25-26 AMP).

"This is my fate in life," she would have reasoned, "the specialists have told me I will never get better, so I will have to learn to live with it." No, this lady knew deep down that she was supposed to be healthy and full of life, that she was supposed to be a conqueror and not a victim. When she heard that Jesus was traveling through her town, something inside her said, "This is your time, this is your moment, this is your due season." She heard what I am telling you today; although she was weak from the loss of blood, and although every thought told her she was wasting her time, she began making her way through the crowd, trying to find Jesus; she was filled with hope, believing that something good was about to happen:

The Bible records this story as we read. "She had heard [reports] about Jesus, and she came up behind Him in the crowd and touched His outer robe. 28 For she thought, "If I just touch His clothing, I will get well." 29 Immediately her flow of blood was dried up; and she felt in her body [and knew without any doubt] that she was healed of her suffering. 30 Immediately Jesus, recognizing in Himself that power had gone out from Him, turned around in the crowd and asked, "Who touched My clothes?" 31 His disciples said to Him, "You see the crowd pressing in around You [from all sides], and You ask, 'Who touched Me?'" 32 Still He kept looking around to see the woman who had done it. 33 And the woman, though she was afraid and trembling, aware of what had happened to her, came and fell down before Him and told Him the whole truth. 34 Then He said to her, "Daughter, your faith [your personal trust and confidence in Me] has restored you to health; go in peace and be [permanently] healed from your suffering." Mark 5:27-34 (AMP)

It attracts God's attention when we live with expectations. We are doing precisely what this lady did by saying throughout the day, "Lord, I think this is my due season, this is my season to accomplish dreams, to break free from this depression, this is my season to meet the right people, this is my season to get healthy and whole." Your faith has the power to move God's hand. What I find fascinating is that Jesus did not heal everyone in the crowd that day; there were other sick people in the crowd, other people in need. This lady, on the other hand, seize her due season with faith; it began in her mind. We should be anticipating things throughout the day. If you are dealing with a disease, you can't afford to keep telling yourself things like, "I don't think I will ever get better, I have had it for so long, I think this is going to be the last of me."

Start speaking to yourself like this lady: "This is my due season to get better." God is restoring my health, and He will complete the number of my days." "This is my due season to come into overflow, to be debt-free, to lend and not borrow," rather than "I will never have enough, I will never get ahead," if you're having financial difficulties. "I am being pursued by blessings. Favor is like a barrier around me. Everything I touch thrives and succeeds." If you are lonely, don't say things like, "I' will never meet the right person because I am too old, I don't have a nice personality, I am not that pretty," or I am not that attractive." "This is my due season of divine encounters for me." God is guiding my steps and putting the proper individuals in my path." Perhaps you had a setback or disappointment sometime past; thinking, "Just my luck, I always get these awful breaks." No, this is your season to see the beauty in the ashes. God is going to utilize what was meant to harm you for your benefit. The most exciting time of your life is immediately ahead of you. You may have experienced a setback, but it was an opportunity for God to do something better.

"Return to your stronghold, O prisoners of hope; today I declare that I will restore to you double". (Zechariah 9:12).

This is the season when you will be able to view twice as much as you did in time past. This is your due season of retribution, repair, and fresh starts. Now is the time to guide your thoughts on the appropriate path. Begin conversing with yourself more constructively. One of the reasons we don't see God's best is that our minds are in a state of neutrality. We are not thinking of anything unpleasant, but we are not releasing our trust; there is no expectancy, just like the other individuals who were near Jesus that day who didn't get healed. God works because of faith. You can be at the right place at the right moment, but you will miss God's best if you are in the wrong frame of mind. This lady was at the right place at the right time when Jesus came by, but unlike the others, she was in the right frame of mind, expecting things to change, expecting to be healed, expecting a breakthrough, and she saw it happen. You are in the right place at the right moment today; God chose you to hear this. Two of the three are already good, but the third is the deciding factor; are you in the appropriate state of mind? Is this your due season?

Right now, Jesus is passing through. He is touched by our faith, not by our numerous needs. He is concerned about our needs. It's easy to believe that "the medical report says I am not going to get better," "my business will never make it," or "this legal matter will never be resolved." No, throw off the doubt and pessimism; you are in the right place at the right time; all you have to do now is get into the proper frame of mind; "Lord, thank you that this is my due season: this is my season to step into leadership, finish school, overcome the addiction, come into overflow, and meet the person of my dreams." If you keep repeating it to yourself, praising God in advance, be prepared for God to show up in your life. He will take you somewhere you couldn't go on your own, opening doors that no one else can close and introducing you to the proper people. He is going to undo what you believed was finished. It will happen out of the blue, unexpectedly, and you will glance up and exclaim, "Wow, I didn't see that coming."

When we hear the expression "I didn't see that coming," it usually refers to anything negative, such as a poor break: "I lost my big client, didn't see it coming." I got a poor medical report, which I didn't expect." "My friend walked out on me, and left me for someone else, I didn't see it coming." But God is going to turn things around in this due season; "I just got a promotion; I didn't see it coming." My child received straight A's in school, which I had not expected. I moved into a lovely new home and had no idea what was in store for me." "I didn't expect my health to improve, and I now feel better than I have in a long time." "Let's give them something to talk about," stated the old country song. God will provide you with something to talk about this year. He will make you a shining example of His goodness. I am sure that lady who was healed after 12 years of illness told everyone who she met, "Let me tell you what the Lord has done for me," and she had enough to talk about.

I am sure you could recall a time in your life when God provided a way when you didn't see one; He placed you in the perfect spot, and you met and fell in love with that person. He shielded your child from the mishap. Even though you were not the most qualified, he offered you the promotion. He was able to turn the situation around. He is providing you with favor for conversation. But, believe me, when I say, you haven't seen anything yet. What God has planned for this due season will be bigger, better, and more gratifying than anything you have seen before. You must prepare yourself; in this due season, you will look up and exclaim, "Wow, I paid off my house, didn't see it coming." "I didn't see that coming, but it broke my addiction." "My family member who used to party all the time, be so wild, now he's coming to church with me, making good decisions, and fulfilling his destiny; sure, "didn't see that coming." According to the Bible: *"Now it shall be, if you diligently listen to and obey the voice of the Lord your God, being careful to do all of His commandments which I am commanding you today, the*

Lord your God will set you high above all the nations of the earth. 2 All these blessings will come upon you and overtake you if you pay attention to the voice of the Lord your God. (Deuteronomy 28:1-2 AMP).

"When you honor God with your life, when you put him first, his blessings will hunt you down and overtake you," the Bible says. We have all had bad things happen to us. Life is unpredictable. But don't fall into the trap of expecting the worst. God is going to flip the tables this due season. You are being pursued by good breaks. Favor, healing, and opportunity are all chasing you down. "To capture by surprise" is one definition of the word "overtake." You could say, "God is going to surprise you," when it says, "God's blessings will overtake you." Suddenly. Unexpectedly. Something unusual. It was a nice respite. It's healing. A raise in pay. This is a divine link. Things that you have been praying about are going to fall into place in this due season. People that are supposed to be there show up. The appropriate circumstances. Something unusual. Unexpectedly. God will provide you with something to talk about.

This is how David put it. *Psalm 27. "Where would I be today if I hadn't thought I'd see God's goodness"?* I'm curious as to how many blessings we're overlooking. How much favor, how much growth are we missing out on because we aren't anticipating it, because we aren't releasing our faith? In effect, David was saying, "Maybe I wouldn't have defeated Goliath if I hadn't believed. Perhaps I would not have ascended to the throne of Israel. When my city of Ziklag was burned down, I may not have been able to reclaim my family and property. What would I be doing now if I hadn't believed? "What are your thoughts on this?

In the scripture, *(1 Samuel 30:1-19 AMP). Now it happened when David and his men came [home] to Ziklag on the third day, [they found] that the Amalekites had made a raid on the Negev (the South country) and on Ziklag, and had overthrown Ziklag and burned it with fire;* ² *and they had taken captive the women [and all] who were there, both small and great. They killed no one, but carried them off [to be used as slaves] and went on their way. ³When David and his men came to the town, it was burned, and their wives and their sons and their daughters had been taken captive. ⁴Then David and the people who were with him raised their voices and wept until [a]they were too exhausted to weep [any longer]. ⁵Now David's two wives had been captured, Ahinoam the Jezreelitess and Abigail the widow of Nabal the Carmelite. ⁶Further, David was greatly distressed because the people spoke of stoning him, for all of them were embittered, each man for his sons and daughters. But David felt strengthened and encouraged in the LORD his God. ⁷David said to Abiathar the priest, Ahimelech's son, "Please bring me the ephod." So Abiathar brought him the ephod. ⁸David inquired of the LORD, saying, "Shall I pursue this band [of raiders]? Will I overtake them?" And He answered him, "Pursue, for you will certainly overtake them, and you will certainly rescue [the captives]." ⁹So David went, he and the six hundred men who were with him, and came to the brook Besor; there those [who could not continue] remained behind. ¹⁰But David pursued [the Amalekites], he and four hundred men, for two hundred who were too exhausted to cross the brook Besor stayed behind. ¹¹They found an Egyptian [who had collapsed] in the field and brought him to David, and gave him bread and he ate, and they gave him water to drink, ¹²and they gave him a piece of a fig cake and two clusters of raisins; and when he had eaten, his [b]energy returned, for he had not eaten bread or had any water to drink for three days and three nights. ¹³David said to him, "To whom do you belong, and where are you from?" He said, "I am a young man from Egypt, a servant of an Amalekite; and my master abandoned me [as useless] when I fell sick three days ago. ¹⁴We made a raid on the Negev of the Cherethites, and on that which belongs to Judah, and on the Negev of Caleb, and we burned Ziklag with fire." ¹⁵Then David said to him, "Will you take me down to this band [of raiders]?" And he said, "Swear to me by God that you will not kill me or turn me over to the hand of my master, and I will bring you down to this band." ¹⁶When he brought David down, the Amalekites had disbanded and spread over all the land, eating and drinking and dancing because of all the great spoil they had taken from the land of the Philistines and from the land of Judah. ¹⁷Then David [and his men] struck them down [in battle] from twilight until the evening of the next day; and not a man of them escaped, except four hundred young men who rode camels and fled. ⁱ⁸ So David recovered all that the Amalekites had taken, and rescued his two wives. ¹⁹ Nothing of theirs was missing whether small or great, sons or daughters, spoil or anything that had been taken; David recovered it all.*

I recall also what the scripture says in *(Psalm 31:19 AMP). How great is Your goodness, Which You have stored up for those who [reverently] fear You, Which You have prepared for those who take refuge in You, Before the sons of man!*

God has blessings in store for people who love the Lord, according to the Scripture. Right now, there are benefits piled up in your name. You have advancement and healing in your future. It's time to have that baby you have been fantasizing about. It was meant to be yours from the beginning. But if you don't believe, you will miss out on God's best if you think like this.
Why wouldn't you try a new tactic and say, "God, I think you want to treat me well. I feel you have some surprises in store for me in the future. I believe this is my due season." God can give you something to talk about if you conduct your life with this expectation. You will glance up and wonder like David did, "Where would I be if I hadn't believed to see God's goodness?"

You must prepare yourselves. God has some surprises in store for you this due season. He is preparing to release some of the benefits he's been holding. It will happen suddenly, unexpectedly, and out of the blue. Friends, you have arrived at the proper location. You have come to the right place at the right moment. I'm requesting that you get into the proper mindset. "Lord, I want to thank you that this is my due season," the lady who touched Jesus said throughout the day. Expect the unexpected. Continue to have faith. Continue to revere God. I believe and declare that if you do it, God will astound you with his goodness. Dreams will come true, promises will be kept, relationships will be mended, favor will be bestowed, and health will be restored, for a new level of your destiny has opened up to you. In the mighty name of our Lord Jesus Christ, Amen.

As a result, I declare today that you will receive your due season according to God's schedule!
Your due season will arrive on time, no matter when it comes.
You have prayed and fasted, and now it's time to celebrate!
You have prayed to the Almighty.
God's Word has been believed and declared by you.
Too many times you have been broke, sick, disheartened, and defeated.
You will have plenty when the time comes.
It has been a difficult period.
It has been difficult to wait.
But God will say, "ENOUGH!" it's your due season.
Your blessings will come to you.
From the north, south, east, and west, I call in your blessings.
Your benefits will arrive when the time is right.
You will be at ease, as no one will be able to scare you.
Your foes will be pursued by you, and they will be slain by the sword before you. God will look favorably at you and bless you with progeny.
Conceive it, trust it, and receive it since your due season is here. Hallelujah!

This book wouldn't be complete without these amazing six Bible characters who figured out what they were created for (and what you can learn about finding your purpose). Let's take one after each.

Solomon, Moses, Paul, Joshua, Jeremiah, and Timothy are six biblical personalities we are familiar with. Of course, God called all of the Scriptural champions to do something. All of their experiences can teach us something. These six have been highlighted because they provide clear examples of how to intentionally find your purpose.

Solomon. Solomon was summoned by God in a dream. "What shall I give you?" God inquired of Solomon. God handed Solomon a blank check and told him to "fill in the amount." Solomon understood that God had called him to be king in place of his father David and that God was willing to give him whatever he desired.

Solomon, on the other hand, was well aware that God was not a fairy godmother or a genie from Aladdin's lamp. He was well aware of the importance of being cautious and not asking for material goods. He requested wisdom and understanding so that he could properly lead the people.

God was pleased with this. As a result, he not only made Solomon a wise leader of the people, but he also granted him the things he could have asked for but didn't. He bestowed wealth onto him, as well as peace from all of his adversaries and a long and fruitful life.

Likewise, when God calls you, he isn't inviting you to this world's material things. God understands you need material things to fulfill your calling, but that is not what you were called to. You have been called by God to assist his people. Working with machines, creating structures, or baking cakes could be your goal. God, on the other hand, is unconcerned with machines, structures, or cakes. He is concerned about those whose lives are made easier by machines. He wants people to be able to live and work in a structure. His objective is to fill people's stomachs with cakes and other delectable foods.

Finding your purpose, whatever God has called you to do, will serve others in the end. You might make money doing it, don't believe God has called you just to be a money maker. He doesn't mind you making money as long as it's not a god to you but ultimately, He has a plan for your life, to worship Him and help others, so think about how you may best serve others.

Moses. Moses, on the other hand, did not begin his writing career by authoring the Bible. He had to first learn to trust God to follow through on his promises. You're most likely familiar with the plot. The Israelites were sold into slavery by Pharaoh. Pharaoh's daughter adopted Moses, who was born an Israelite. He responded and murdered the Egyptian and to evade the punishment of the crime, chose to flee.

Moses married a Midianite girl and worked as a shepherd for his father-in-sheep law after fleeing Egypt. One day he noticed a bush on fire, but it did not burn. From a blazing bush, God spoke to him. "Return to Egypt," as God instructed him. Moses would be used by God to set the Israelites free from slavery.

Moses believed it would be a good idea to debate with God instead of saying, "Yes, sir!" and fleeing to Egypt. He came up with every reason he could think of to explain why his plan wouldn't work. "I'm not the right guy." "The Israelites will not believe that I had a conversation with God." "I am not a gifted orator." "I'm sure there's someone else you could send." Moses couldn't believe God was going to use him. God had called him to a mission that he couldn't possibly fulfill.

God became enraged with Moses after a long period of silence. Do not irritate God when he summons you. Keep in mind who he is and what he is capable of. *" But he said, "What is impossible with man is possible with God". (Luke 18:27 ESV).* Is it seeming tough to find your purpose? Allow him to test your faith and trust in him.

Paul. People were called by God not just in the Old Testament, but also in the New Testament. Take a look at Paul's goal. Through Ananias, God summoned Paul. The story is told in the 9th chapter of Acts. *"But the Lord said to him, "Go, for he is a chosen vessel of Mine to bear My name before Gentiles, kings,* *and the children[a] of Israel. For I will show him how many things he must suffer for My name's sake.' (Acts 9:15-16 NKJV).*

For the sake of the gospel, God called Paul to suffer. The one who was persecuting became the one who was being persecuted. However, despite the difficulties, Paul learned to be content. *"Rejoice in the Lord constantly,"* he wrote from a Roman prison. *"Rejoice once more!" (Philippians 4:4).*

How can one maintain such a positive attitude in the face of adversity? Paul knew he was only going to be in pain for a short time. *"For our present troubles are small and won't last very long. Yet they produce for us a glory that vastly outweighs them and will last forever! So we don't look at the troubles we can see now; rather, we fix our gaze on things that cannot be seen. For the things we see now will soon be gone, but the things we cannot see will last forever." (2 Corinthians 4:17-18 NLT).*

Finding your mission, on the other hand, has eternal ramifications. It won't only have an impact on this world. People will be affected by your mission for the rest of their lives. Except for those things that have eternal repercussions, everything we do in this life will be a distant memory one day. If God calls us to a transitory goal, we must question if we are hearing God correctly.

Joshua. God appointed a new leader for the people of Israel when Moses, the Lord's servant, died. Joshua was summoned to take command. God told Joshua to follow the law that Moses had written down, even though Moses had been the spokesman for God previously. *" Be strong and very courageous. Be careful to obey all the law my servant Moses gave you; do not turn from it to the right or to the left, that you may be successful wherever you go" (Joshua 1:7 NIV).*

By following the Book of the Law, the only Bible available to him, Joshua flourished and completed God's goal. Similarly, we fulfill God's plan for us by adhering to the truth he has previously revealed through the law, prophets, gospels, and the rest of the Bible. Anything that agrees with the Bible is true, whereas anything that contradicts the revealed truth is not from God.

The Bible is a great place to start when looking for God's purpose for you. If you desire to know and follow God's will, you should read the scriptures regularly, just like the Bereans did, to ensure that what you think you know is correct.

Jeremiah. *"Do not be afraid of their faces,"* God warned Jeremiah when he was summoned. *"Be not afraid of them, for I am with you to deliver you, says the LORD. (Jeremiah 1:8- RSV)*. Jeremiah must have forgotten about this caveat years later. He was chastised for his "doom and gloom" predictions. Finally, he came up with an idea. "What if I just don't tell them what the Lord is telling me?" "What if I simply don't tell them what the Lord is telling me?" This, however, did not work. *"If I say, "I will not remember Him Or speak His name anymore, "Then my heart becomes a burning fire Shut up in my bones. And I am weary of enduring and holding it in; I cannot endure it [nor contain it any longer]." (Jeremiah 20:9 AMP)*.

Don't assume you can ignore finding your purpose if God asks you to accomplish something and it gets difficult. God will not let you off the hook so easily. Be prepared for your bones to combust if you decide to tell God, "Nope!" You won't be able to find serenity until you choose to obey God. It's probably better if you simply go ahead and do it.

Timothy. Timothy, Paul's protégé, is the subject of our final biblical character study. The imparting of spiritual talents through the laying on of hands was his call to purpose. In Paul's first letter to him, we learn about his call. *"Do not neglect the spiritual gift that is in you, which was given to you when the prophets spoke and the elders laid their hands on you." (1 Timothy 4:14 GNT)*.

In Timothy's second letter, Paul also mentions this episode, which I believe is the same one. *"For this reason, I remind you to keep alive the gift that God gave you when I laid my hands on you." (2 Timothy 1:6 GNT)*.

Paul and Silas traveled to Lystra and Derbe on their second missionary expedition. They discovered Timothy there, and it was shown to them what his future significance would be. Paul and Silas gathered the elders of the church and prophesied over Timothy by placing their hands on him. The young man received a spiritual gift as the Holy Spirit descended upon him. He became a gospel preacher and Paul's spiritual son.

Peter additionally says that each of us has a spiritual gift. *"God has given each of you a gift from his great variety of spiritual gifts. Use them well to serve one another." (1 Peter 4:10 NLT)*. Each person's mission, or calling, is determined by the gift they have received from God. The method you are to minister to the body of Christ, His church, is to find your mission by discovering His spiritual gift(s).

To sum up, discovering your purpose is essential. Everyone who is a Christian has a calling, a mission, or a ministry. We shall discover our purpose as we read and focus on the Bible, much as Joshua did. Our mission will necessitate faith, just as Moses' did. God will make us uneasy, just as he did Jeremiah until we go out to fulfill our destiny. Our goal, like Solomon's, will be to help others rather than to acquire possessions. Our genuine mission, like Paul's, will have eternal significance, and, like Timothy, God has equipped us with the skills we need to fulfill it.

Jesus said, "Ask, and you will receive; seek, and you will find; knock, and the door will be opened to you.," (Matthew 7:7 GNT). Allow me to urge you to ask God to reveal his plan for your life. And when he does, resolve to submit to his will and walk in the direction he directs you.

May your life leap as you make every effort in **Living the Intentional Life**. God's blessings!

Then I will give you rain in due season, and the land shall yield her increase, and the trees of the field shall yield their fruit. (Leviticus 26:4 KJV).

HALLELUJAH!

NOTE

NOTE

Made in the USA
Columbia, SC
24 May 2023